D0049326

THE BLUEBIRD CAFE SCRAPBOOK

THE BLUEBIRD CAFE SCRAPBOOK

MUSIC & MEMORIES FROM NASHVILLE'S LEGENDARY SINGER-SONGWRITER SHOWCASE

EDITED BY AMY KURLAND, MARK BENNER & NEIL FAGAN

HarperEntertainment
An Imprint of HarperCollins*Publishers*

HarperCollins books may be purchased for educational, business, or sales promotional use. For information please write: Special Markets Department, HarperCollins Publishers Inc., 10 East 53rd Street, New York, NY 10022.

FIRST EDITION

Printed on acid-free paper

Designed by Adrian Leichter

Library of Congress Cataloging-in-Publication Data
Kurland, Amy.
    The Bluebird Cafe scrapbook / Amy Kurland.
       p. cm.
    ISBN 0-06-093521-9
       1. Bluebird Cafe (Restaurant: Nashville, Tenn.)—Anniversaries, etc.—Miscellanea.
    2. Country Music—Tennessee—Nashville—History and criticism—Miscellanea.
    3. Country Musicians—Tennessee—Nashville—Anecdotes. 4. Cookery, American.
    I. Title

    TX945.5.B58 K87 2002
    647.9576855—dc21
                                                                    2001051748

02 03 04 05 06 ❖/RRD 10 9 8 7 6 5 4 3 2 1

■ ■ ■

For performers, New York City has Carnegie Hall.

Los Angeles has the Hollywood Bowl.

London has the Royal Albert Hall.

Nashville has the Ryman Auditorium.

For the past twenty years, thank God, songwriters have had the Bluebird Cafe.

This book is a myriad of stories about the songs these songwriters have created. It truly is the Mecca for all songwriters.

Thanks, Amy, for giving all these songs a home.

VINCE GILL

■ ■ ■

Contents

CONTENTS

THE BLUEBIRD CAFE SCRAPBOOK

A BRIEF HISTORY
OF NASHVILLE

Don't worry, there won't be a test.

Mention Nashville to almost anyone around the world, and the first thing that comes to mind is country music. It is, however, a relatively new industry in the city, which was established on Christmas Day 1779. Nashville grew and prospered, and became the permanent capital of Tennessee in 1843. In the second half of the nineteenth century the city came to be known as the "Athens of the South" as schools such as Vanderbilt, Fisk, Meharry, Belmont, and Peabody were founded. Nashville is also the home of two former presidents: Andrew Jackson and James K. Polk.

During the Civil War, Nashville was a strategic stronghold, given its location on the Cumberland River, and was heavily contested by both armies. After the war the city's growth continued. Printing and publishing, much of it religion-oriented, became important industries, followed by insurance and medicine. The insurance industry played a role in steering Nashville down the path that would one day lead it to be nicknamed "Music City." In 1925 the National Life and Accident Insurance Company launched the radio station WSM and made it the home of *The Grand Ole Opry*. In 1926 WLAC was established by the Life and Casualty Insurance Company of Tennessee.

It wasn't until the mid-forties, however, that Nashville began to blossom as a recording-industry town. RCA and Decca sent executives from New York to roll tape on Eddy Arnold and Red Foley respectively. Soon they were opening their own studios and were followed by several smaller independent labels such as Bullet, Dot, Nashboro, Excello, and Republic. As the recording industry grew, related businesses began to pop up, including booking agencies, music publishing houses, and A & R (artists and repertoire) offices. Many of these businesses clustered together on a few blocks of Sixteenth and Seventeenth avenues between Belmont College and Vanderbilt University, and the area became known as Music Row.

In the early seventies, Opryland USA appeared to the east of downtown, on land purchased by NLT, the parent company of National Life Insurance and *The Grand Ole Opry*. Over the years, the complex has grown to include the Opryland Hotel, the New Opry House, and a theme park complete with roller-coasters and musical revues. The Nashville Network and WSM studios are also housed there. In 1983 the entire complex was purchased by the Gaylord Broadcasting Company. The theme park has since been dismantled.

The roller-coasters may be gone at Opryland, but for country music the ride continues. Over the last forty years there have been plenty of ups and downs, both commercially and critically. The Nashville Sound, Honky-Tonk, Urban Cowboy, New Traditionalist, and New Country are just some of the names given to the trends in country, but the biggest trend of the last decade can be summed up in a single name: Garth. Not only did Garth Brooks take country music to the masses in a way no one before him even thought possible, he's also become the top-selling male artist in the history of the music industry, toppling Elvis Presley and Billy Joel and threatening to outsell even the Beatles. Soon after Garth showed it could be done, several other country acts were seeing their albums sell by the millions. Brooks & Dunn, Billy Ray Cyrus, Tim McGraw, LeAnn Rimes, Shania Twain, and the Dixie Chicks are part of that platinum club.

Good times for country music have meant good times for Nashville. The last decade has seen unprecedented growth for the city. A new arena and the complete resurgence of the downtown area were just the beginning. Both the NFL and the NHL have staked a claim in Music City with the Tennessee Titans and the Nashville Predators, respectively. Manufacturing has expanded in the area with the arrival of Nissan and Saturn factories as well as a new Dell Computers facility.

While country may be king in Nashville, on any given night you can find virtually any style of music in the dozens of nightclubs, listening rooms, and lounges that dot the city. Just as there are residents of Orlando, Florida, who've never been to Disney World, there are still plenty of people in Nashville oblivious to the goings-on along Music Row. Nashville today means many different things to many different people. Call it the Athens of the South, the Protestant Vatican, or Music City, chances are you'll find whatever you're looking for in Nashville, Tennessee.

A BRIEF HISTORY
OF COUNTRY MUSIC

(Very Brief, Really Short)

Long before there was the Bluebird Cafe, the Grand Ole Opry, or even Nashville itself, there were music and songwriters. Songs are probably as old as speech. Adam and Eve might well have sung "Don't Sit Under the Apple Tree with Anyone Else but Me" until they were kicked out of the garden due to their poor dietary choices. Centuries

This picture hung over the Bluebird stage for many years before Gove Scrivenor made the trademark neon sign for us.

later, in Europe and elsewhere, traveling troubadours rode from town to town, telling the news, usually through song, and spreading songs throughout the land. Music has always been the universal language.

The history of American music began in Europe. Immigrants brought with them their traditional hymns and folk songs, jigs and reels, ballads and lullabies. In the new land the violin, which dates back to pre-Renaissance days, became the fiddle, and accordions or squeeze boxes were handed down from generation to generation. Mandolins, banjos, and guitars of all shapes and sizes were part of the entertainment mix.

As America grew, so did its repertoire and its musical styles. Irish, Scottish, Spanish, German, Italian, Slavic, French, and even African sounds were being blended in communities across the country. The term "melting pot" applied not only to the various nationalities that made up America but to the music that was being created as well.

The roots of country music are in the songs of the Appalachian Mountains. But with each move west, some new song style was born. Once the settlers reached the Mississippi, songs specifically celebrating that magnificent river and the boats that would travel her sprang up. Three cities founded on the banks of the Mississippi—New Orleans, Memphis, and St. Louis—would play a significant role in the development of jazz and blues. Farther west, as towns like Abilene, Texas; Cheyenne, Wyoming; and Tombstone, Arizona, were popping up, so did a new American icon, the cowboy. And he too had a song to sing.

In the latter half of the 1800s, musical theater was the prominent source of entertainment in East Coast cities such as Boston, Philadelphia, and especially New York. That period also gave America its first songwriting superstar. Stephen Foster's credits include "Oh! Susanna," "Camptown Races," and "My Old Kentucky Home," among many others.

In early August 1927, Ralph Peer, scouting talent for the Victor Recording Company of New York, rolled in to Bristol, Tennessee, in the mountains of Appalachia, hoping to record some rural or "hillbilly" music. Among those he auditioned were the Carters, known as the First Family of Country Music, and Jimmie Rodgers. Sisters Sara and Maybelle Carter and Sara's husband, A. P., recorded numerous tracks with Peer, including "Wildwood Flower," "Keep on the Sunny

Side," and "Will the Circle Be Unbroken." Rodgers recorded two songs, "Sleep, Baby, Sleep" and "The Soldier's Sweetheart." Thus the first country recordings were made.

Both the Carter Family and Rodgers have influenced virtually every country artist who came after them. Their songs, both traditional and original, created a sound that still has the power to move listeners today. They made the first nationally popular records of the genre, and Bristol is often referred to as the Birthplace of Country Music.

The phonograph player and the latest modern marvel, radio, made it possible for country music to reach the highest mountain and the deepest "holler." Radio stations were going on air from coast to coast and they began broadcasting musical variety shows that would become known as "barn dances" or jamborees. Chicago's WLS aired what became the prototype for nearly all the shows that followed: the *WLS Barn Dance*. Similar shows aired in Knoxville and Nashville, utilizing local musicians as well as those that would travel from city to city to appear on the radio. But it was Nashville's clear-channel fifty-thousand-watt radio station WSM that launched what would become the longest-running radio show in the world. Signing on in November 1925, two years before Mr. Peer's search for hillbilly music, *WSM Barn Dance* became an instant success and was officially renamed *The Grand Ole Opry* in December 1928. Early *Opry* stars included Jimmy Thompson, who played the very first notes on the air, Uncle Dave Macon, and the Crook Brothers.

Broadcast from the WSM studios in downtown Nashville, *The Grand Ole Opry* attracted such large audiences that the station built larger studios, and the crowds kept coming. After outgrowing Studios B and C, the radio show moved to the Hillsboro Theater (now the Belcourt) in 1934. Two years later it relocated to the Dixie Tabernacle in East

The father of bluegrass, Bill Monroe, delights the Bluebird crowd with his signature sound.

Nashville, then to the new War Memorial Auditorium back in downtown in 1939. Four years later the show moved again, to the Ryman Auditorium, where it remained for thirty-one years until the New Grand Ole Opry House was opened at Opryland USA in 1974.

The Grand Ole Opry's first true star was Roy Acuff, who joined the

cast in February 1938. Acuff, now referred to as the Garth Brooks of his day, was known then as the King of Country Music. Bill Monroe, inducted in October 1939, brought bluegrass music to the Opry stage, and in 1940 Minnie Pearl provided the comic relief. The success of *The Grand Ole Opry* spawned a secondary business in Nashville—the music industry. With all the artists gathering in Nashville for weekend performances on the *Opry*, it made sense for them to live in the city and do their business there.

In 1942 Roy Acuff teamed with pianist and songwriter Fred Rose to form Acuff-Rose Music. Acuff had been selling songbooks on the radio, and after he had gone through ten thousand books he realized that establishing a publishing operation would be in his best interest. Rose, who came from Chicago but also knew the music business in New York, was able to get songs recorded outside of Nashville. Acuff, now the star of the *Opry*, would steer talented songwriters to Rose. One singer-songwriter Acuff sent off to see Fred Rose was Hank Williams. Signed to a publishing contract in 1946, Williams is still considered to be the best songwriter country music has ever seen or heard.

With the success of Acuff-Rose, other music-related ventures opened their doors in Nashville. Publishing companies and recording studios began popping up all over town. While most of the early recording sessions in Nashville took place at the WSM studios and other radio stations, Owen Bradley, a piano player and arranger for WSM, decided to establish his own studio. Bradley pur-

BLUE MONDAYS

Monday. Look it up in the dictionary, and the definition will read: "the slowest night in bar business." Ask any bar owner and they'll tell you it's true. So, in the mid-eighties, when bassist Dave Pomeroy approached Amy about an idea he had for "Blue Mondays," she jumped on it. When it comes to that first night of the week, anything is worth a shot. Thus began a tradition of Monday-night blues at the 'Bird that continues today.

Blue Monday was not only an idea, it was a band. In addition to Pomeroy on bass, there was also Rogie Ray on harmonica, Eddie Blakely and Billy Earl McClelland on guitars, Johnny Neel on keyboards, and Jimmy Greasy on sax. They all shared vocals. While the first set usually consisted of originals, the second set turned into an all-out jam session, with guests frequently sitting in. Vince Gill, Wynonna, and Dave Olney were all popular drop-ins during this time. Blue Monday played almost every Monday at the Bluebird for about four years. They also recorded an album during this time, but eventually the group disbanded to follow separate career directions.

Although Blue Monday ended, blues on Mondays did not. A tall, lanky fellow from Missouri named Mike Henderson had recently come to town and was lookin' to play. In 1986 he formed the Kingsnakes along with guitarist Kenny Greenberg, keyboardist Wally Wilson, bassist Glen Worf, and drummer Bill Swartz. James Stroud eventually replaced Swartz on drums. With the two-guitar attack of Henderson and Greenberg, the band was an instant hit. One was a blistering blues/slide player, the other a rock-and-roll explosion. Glen Worf summed up their

chased a piece of land on Sixteenth Avenue South, a few blocks west of downtown, and erected a post–World War II Quonset hut, filled it with recording gear, and made history as the first music venture on what would become Nashville's famed Music Row. The site of Bradley's studio is now Sony Music, a building that literally enveloped the original Quonset hut. However, if you go behind the Sony building and stand in the parking lot, you can still see a trace of the original curve of the hut roof.

With the artists living in Nashville, recording in Nashville, and now being published in Nashville, it only made sense that record labels established offices in the fledgling Music City. Capitol and Decca were early arrivals, followed by Columbia and Victor (which would become RCA). Independent labels such as Republic, Bullet, and Dot were also competing for talent and airtime. In addition to all of the country music being recorded in Nashville, African-American music maintained a strong presence especially due to the success of the Fisk University Jubilee Singers. Nashboro and the subsidiary label Excello were created to record the region's black talent in the fields of gospel and R & B respectively.

In the early 1950s Nashville was the center of the universe for country music. Acuff was still a huge star, and new performers like Hank Snow, Little Jimmie Dickens, Hank Thompson, Faron Young, Webb Pierce, and Ernest Tubb were all selling records and touring constantly. Kitty Wells created the first million-selling single, "It Wasn't God Who Made Honky Tonk Angels," which was produced by Owen

BLUE MONDAYS

sound fittingly: "a rock-and-roll bottom with blues on top."

Monday nights were now ruled by the Kingsnakes. You had to get there early because the room got so full they'd eventually close off the door before the band even played a note. The buzz reached the head honchos on Music Row, and the Kingsnakes were soon signed to a deal with Curb Records. Before their debut album came out they had to shorten their name to the Snakes due to the number of other bands with the Kingsnake moniker. The album rocked, but as it so often happens in the music biz, quality doesn't always translate into units sold. Stroud started producing more and more acts, Wilson was tapped for an executive position at MCA, and it just got harder and harder to hold the band together. The Snakes eventually slithered into the history books.

Henderson saw the end before it happened, and before the Snakes had played their last gig he had a new band ready to take its place. With Worf still holding down the low end, Mike recruited ace drummer John Gardner, and the Bluebloods were born. In a three-piece combo, Henderson was able to really stretch out on his slide guitar and harmonica. The 'Bloods became so popular that other musicians were practically begging to sit in. When they expanded to a foursome with the addition of keyboards, the first ivory tickler to fill the spot was none other than legendary piano man Al Kooper, best known for his work with Bob Dylan and for founding Blood, Sweat and Tears. When he left, Greg Wetzel took over the keys for a while before they landed Reese Wynans, a recent Nashville transplant from Austin. Reese stayed on long

(continued)

7

Bradley. All was right with the world until the day that rock and roll hit the airwaves. In middecade, country music nosedived. Sales were off, radio stations were switching formats, and rock and roll was the new king of the airwaves.

BLUE MONDAYS

enough to record the 'Bloods' first album, appropriately titled *First Blood*. He wasn't available to tour as much as the band wanted, so he too bowed out, and John Jarvis took over. The line-up has been rock-solid since then, and the band has recorded a second album, *Thicker Than Water.* Both albums are available on the Dead Reckoning label, which was the brainchild of Henderson and fellow Nashville mavericks Kieran Kane, Kevin Welch, Tammy Rogers, and Harry Stinson.

The Bluebloods have represented the blues and Nashville at several blues festivals and even kicked butt in New York when they beat out Al Kooper's new group in a "Battle of the Bands" at the Bottom Line. We like to see them get out there and spread the word, but we like it even better when they come home. Mondays will always mean the blues at the Bluebird.

In an effort to counter the success of that new music, the "Nashville Sound" was created. Owen Bradley, who was running Decca Records, and Chet Atkins, the head of RCA, both began to make records that would mute the steel guitar, fiddle, and banjo and add string arrangements in an effort to urbanize the sound. Bradley found success by utilizing the new formula on Patsy Cline's hits "Crazy," "I Fall to Pieces," and "Walkin' After Midnight." At RCA Atkins created similar recordings with Jim Reeves and Eddy Arnold, all with a lot less twang.

In 1958 the Country Music Association was formed to promote the genre (and to an extent combat rock and roll) throughout the country and around the world. Within ten years it would become one of the most powerful trade groups in the entire music industry. In 1961 it established the Country Music Hall of Fame. The first three inductees were Hank Williams, Jimmie Rodgers, and Fred Rose. A year later Roy Acuff would become the first living inductee. The CMA created its own awards show in 1967 and continues to spread the country-music word.

Folk music predates country and rock and continues to influence both. Folk's biggest impact came during the 1960s with the arrival of Bob Dylan. Like the ancient troubadour, his songs were the headlines of the times, and the times were "a-changin' " indeed. Johnny Cash was the first prominent Nashville artist to champion and befriend Dylan. "It Ain't Me, Babe" was a hit for Cash in 1965. The following year Dylan's landmark album *Blonde on Blonde* was recorded on Music Row and forever changed the perception of recording in Nashville.

Joining Dylan in the folk revival were such artists and writers as Joan Baez (who had introduced Dylan to her audiences), Ian & Sylvia, Tim Hardin, Tom Paxton, Pete Seeger, Buffy Sainte-Marie, and the Kingston Trio. Almost all of them had their songs covered by Nashville's top vocalists in the sixties.

Songwriters began gravitating to Nashville by the early sixties, and music publishing was big business. Roger Miller began his writing and recording career during this period, and Harlan Howard ("Busted") also hit his stride.

The late great Roger Miller shares his witty ditties with a Bluebird crowd.

The husband-and-wife songwriting team of Felice and Boudleaux Bryant ("Wake Up, Little Suzie," "Rocky Top") continued to create pop and country hits, having written numerous hits for the Everly Brothers since the late fifties. Marijohn Wilkin ("One Day at a Time") along with Don Gibson ("Oh, Lonesome Me" and "I Can't Stop Loving You") were a few of the early writers getting cuts on Music Row.

Country artists making an impact in the 1960s included Loretta Lynn, Porter Wagoner, Marty Robbins, Bill Anderson, Jack Greene, Sonny James, Ferlin Husky, Leroy Van Dyke, the Louvin Brothers, Billy Walker, Johnny & Jack, George Jones, Glen Campbell, and Chet Atkins. While some of them would write their own hits, the songwriting community began to flourish with newcomers like Tom T. Hall ("Harper Valley PTA"), Curly Putnam and Bobby Braddock ("D.I.V.O.R.C.E."), Dallas Frazier ("There Goes My Everything"), and Bobby Russell ("Honey").

Tom T. Hall makes a rare live appearance and to make it even more special he's joined by R. B. Morris (center) and Billy Joe Shaver.

The music would get a little stirred up in the 1970s when Willie Nelson, Waylon Jennings, Tompall Glaser, and others would rebel from the Nashville system and make records in their own style. Often these artists would use their touring band to make records rather than the Nashville session musicians. Kris Kristofferson churned out hit songs and his own albums during this period. But the majority of the recording artists still looked to Nashville's top publishing houses for songs and writers like Don Wayne ("Country Bumpkin"), Ben Peters ("Before the Next Teardrop Falls"), Kenny O'Dell ("Behind Closed Doors"), Bob McDill ("Amanda"), Roger Bowling ("Lucille"), and Sonny Throckmorton ("Wish I Was 18 Again"), who continued to provide the hits. Newcomer Don Schlitz got his first cut in the latter part of the decade, when Kenny Rogers recorded his song "The Gambler," which became a huge hit, winning a Grammy and a CMA Award for Song of the Year in 1979.

Ricky Skaggs keeps it country.

Thoughout the seventies and into the eighties, country music saw its popularity ebb and flow. It rose with the "Urban Cowboy" craze of the early eighties and then subsequently fell when everything began to sound like bland, middle-of-the-road fare. While artists like Merle Haggard, George Jones, and Willie Nelson were keeping it country, Alabama, Anne Murray, and Kenny Rogers were blurring the lines between pop and country, all the while selling millions of records. While the country-music industry was mired in strings and pop fascinations, Ricky Skaggs quietly released "Waitin' for the Sun to Shine" on Epic Records in 1981. The album was hard-core country, and the single "I Don't Care" (written by Webb Pierce and Cindy Walker) spent a week at number one in July 1982. Skaggs would begin a streak of hits on the country charts that would include "Heartbroke," "Crying My Heart Out Over You," "Highway 40 Blues," "Honey (Open That Door)," "I Wouldn't Change You If I Could," and "Uncle Pen," which featured bluegrass legend Bill Monroe.

While Skaggs was on his tear, a former dishwasher at the Nashville Palace would give country music a second shot in the arm, artistically and financially. With hits like "On the Other Hand,"

"1982," and "Forever and Ever Amen," Randy Travis helped to launch the "New Traditionalist" movement, selling well over ten million records in his first five years.

Unlike Skaggs, who came from a bluegrass background, Travis was steeped in traditional country music, and the two performers are credited with making country music country again. Following in their footsteps were George Strait, Dwight Yoakam, and Keith Whitley.

Every now and then wires get crossed and a double booking occurs. It happened one night with Carlene Carter. Fortunately for us, she split the night with Mary Chapin Carpenter.

By the end of the eighties still more traditional artists were making hit records—Clint Black, Alan Jackson, and Steve Earle. And then Garth hit. And hit and hit and hit. A performer drawn equally to Billy Joel and George Strait, Garth Brooks not only broke all the records in country music, he broke all the records, period. After his lead, more and more country artists saw their albums sell in the multiple millions. Younger listeners tuned in, and country radio surpassed rock in the Arbitron ratings.

Garth's success was phenomenal. In the span of just a little over ten years he has sold more than 100 million albums. Only the Beatles have sold more. His tours were high-energy rock-and-roll-type shows, but his music and his message were country. He is credited with saving the country format, and during his unbelievable run, all was right in Nashville. The record labels, music publishers, booking agents, and managers all made money. The boom was staggering, and if a record company operated one label, it quickly launched a second to try to get a bigger piece of the pie. At one time in the mid-1990s, Nashville was home to some twenty-six record labels, all of which were owned at the time by five conglomerate label groups. The good times were better than ever. And of course, the record labels tried to mimic the Garth Brooks success

Mary Chapin Carpenter (left) yucks it up with Jon Vezner, Kathy Mattea, and Tim O'Brien.

with more "hat acts." Few had Brooks's charisma, however, and country was flooded with a lot of generic hunks. In a way, that might have been a good thing, for the last decade has seen the emergence of an incredible number of strong female voices, among them Reba McEntire, Patty Loveless, Mary Chapin Carpenter, Alison Krauss, Faith Hill, Trisha Yearwood, LeAnn Rimes, and Shania Twain.

The door to a thousand dreams? Maybe so. On their first visit, however, most people are amazed to see how small and unassuming the Bluebird Cafe looks.

Unfortunately, near the end of the decade Garth quit touring, record labels were finding it harder and harder to break new acts, radio was consolidating at an alarming rate, and only a handful of artists were selling millions and millions of records. The new labels that were started just a few years earlier were just as quickly closed. Radio was playing more pop-oriented artists like Shania Twain, Faith Hill, and LeAnn Rimes, who were succeeding on both the country and the pop charts, and the old argument about "keeping it real," "keeping it country," and "remembering your roots" had resumed.

Three chords and the truth. America's music. The songs of the working man. Whatever you call it, country music is rich in history and tradition. It's organic. It's constantly growing and changing, and for hundreds of songwriters, Nashville is the one place where the song is still king.

The Bluebird Cafe opened its doors to songwriters in 1982. In the following chapters you will find some Bluebird memories from some of the most prominent songwriters of the eighties and nineties. These are writers who grew up listening to Lennon and McCartney, Don Henley, and Ray Davies as well as Hank Williams, Harlan Howard, and Don Gibson, men and women who frequently perform at the Bluebird Cafe and have had a hand in changing the landscape of Nashville songwriting.

THE BLUEBIRD'S HUMBLE BEGINNING

Or, How to Create an Institution Without Really Planning To

It was just supposed to be a casual gourmet restaurant for the ladies who lunch after shopping the affluent boutiques of Green Hills, the upscale neighborhood southwest of downtown Nashville. Then someone suggested having a little live music. Thus, an empire was born. Well, a world-famous listening room, anyway.

No one knew what was about to bloom in the tiny little strip mall in the Green Hills area of Nashville. Especially us.

Amy Kurland, owner of the Bluebird Cafe, had attended a cooking school in Washington, D.C., and was now back in Nashville ready to put her new knowledge to use. With a small inheritance from her grandmother, she started looking for the right location to open a restaurant. She found it in a closed-down game room in a small strip mall on Hillsboro Road. It was away from Music Row and the downtown club scene, but that didn't seem to matter. Live music at the Bluebird was an immediate success, especially performing songwriters.

Amy Kurland

I am often asked why I started the Bluebird Cafe. People believe that I must have had a brilliant business plan and wonderful business skills. I must confess that the Bluebird Cafe happened because of three of my vices. Yes, I had always wanted to open my own restaurant, because I grew up in Nashville,

Before Amy made it the Bluebird Cafe, 4104 Hillsboro Road was the home to many establishments, including the Green Hills Game Room.

where good, independent restaurants were rare. But mostly the Blue-bird came about because of my interest in food, drink, and guitar players.

For a very short time in the late 1970s there was a great bar called J. Austin's, located in the basement of the property that is now the

Dave Billings enjoys the roomy comfort of our first men's room.

Bluebird. It was a wonderful room for music and a great hangout. Some of the regulars who performed there were Pebble Daniel, Pat McLaughlin, and Dave Olney. I went there a lot, with my guitar-player boyfriend. I was not long out of college, and not sure what to do next. But I had always said I wanted to open a restaurant, and I had a little bit of money that I inherited from my grandmother.

So Jerry and I would hang out at J. Austin's, and I told a few people that I wanted to go into the restaurant business. One of the bartenders there, the great Bob White, wanted to get into the business with me.

Amy (far left) with some of the earliest friends and employees of the Bluebird. Okay, we fired the kid due to child labor laws.

He said that the restaurant would need a bar and that we should have live music there, too.

I was young and naïve, and it all sounded like a lot of fun. So I started scouting for a location for this restaurant with bar and stage. I looked at a place near 100 Oaks Mall (too small) and one out off Highway 100 (too grubby). Then one day, riding through my own neighborhood, I spotted a FOR LEASE sign in the window of the local game room. That location was very familiar to me. When I was ten years old or so, my mother volunteered at Circle Theatre, a neighborhood theater group. While she painted sets and built props, my sister, my brother, and I often waited for her at the counter of Yates Pharmacy. The space had since been a pizza parlor (the Red Geranium) and a sewing machine store.

With my father's help, I took possession of the storefront at 4104 Hillsboro Road and got ready to open my own business. Some of the great musicians who would later play the Bluebird stage helped to build it. Ralph Vitello, Kitty Wolf, Frank Sheen, and many others came over to paint the walls and fix up the kitchen.

I changed a lot once the Bluebird became a reality. Over time I got serious about running this business. I was determined not to fail. I had opened the club with many good friends on the payroll, tending bar, cooking, waitressing. Some of those people turned out to be better friends than employees. I realized how much I didn't know about running a business and took some small-business classes at Nashville Tech. I took advice from some people and ignored advice from others. And twenty years later, we're still here. Not because I ever dreamed this up or wrote a business plan but because the Bluebird was meant to be. It is the combined effort of hundreds of great waitresses, cooks, and dishwashers, of thousands of devoted songwriters, guitar players, and musicians, as well as the tens of thousands of music-loving customers. The Bluebird Cafe has become a home to songwriters and a really great way for me to spend my time.

■　■　■　■　■

Amy Kurland is the owner of the Bluebird Cafe. She was born in Tulsa, Oklahoma, and grew up in Ithaca, New York. She graduated from George Washington University with a double major in American literature and American studies. She lives in Nashville with her dogs, Shasta, Daisy, and Puzzle.

Sheldon Kurland (Amy's Father)

When Amy was looking for a location for a restaurant she wanted to open, she actually asked for my advice. "Not there," I said, when she was considering a deserted building on Sixteenth Avenue. "Nobody will come at night. After nine P.M. it is a dead planet, and people and you will be sorry." What I was actually thinking was that she would be closing up very late and be by herself on a godforsaken street except for a few

Despite the well-meaning advice from her dad, Sheldon Kurland (pictured here with Barbara Kurland, Amy's mom), Amy thought people might actually enjoy hearing music while they dined.

(heavens to Betsy) recording musicians. Then she found a place on Route 70 South that looked even more unsafe for my little girl. "It will be harder to get customers here than on Music Row." In fact every location looked like "Eaters won't come."

And then she found the dead body of the old Yates Pharmacy, which had become a Red Geranium and then a game room. It was very close to the (upscale) Green Hills Mall and on old, safe Hillsboro Road. Without even looking at the inside of the building I whole-heartedly gave my approval.

Everything was working out fine until I noticed she was having a raised platform put in one part of the floor. "Why are you building a stage?" I asked.

"So I can have people play and sing," she answered.

Then I gave her my greatest piece of advice. "Trust me, people don't want to hear live music while they're eating."

■　■　■　■　■

Before Amy Kurland made a name for herself as the owner of the Bluebird Cafe, her father, Sheldon Kurland, was making a name for himself as the founder of the Shelly Kurland Strings, one of the most sought-after groups for sessions along Music Row.

First it was writers onstage. Then it was writers in the round. Finally, it was writers at the bar. We suspect that's what they (Vince Gill and Don Schlitz) wanted all along.

Bruce Burch

I have only played the Bluebird on one occasion, since, as Amy Kurland can attest, I am a songwriter but I certainly am no singer. You see, Amy and I go back long before the Bluebird flew. Amy's mother, Barbara Kurland, was one of the pioneers of Second Avenue's development. Barbara converted a warehouse on the corner of Second Avenue and Church Street into an entertainment/shopping venue, opening Goodies Warehouse back when the Hard Rock Cafe was just a pebble in a parking lot. Goodies was an eclectic mix of artist workshops, clothing and gift emporiums, and restaurants. I first met Amy when she opened a bakery there. I was a "perspiring" songwriter, and my means of support at that early stage of my career was operating a classy joint known as the Saucy Dog, also in the "warehouse." Actually, the Dog was basically a glorified hot dog stand.

Amy generally closed up the bakery after the lunch rush, when everybody had bought all the sweets they were going to buy for the day. I, being the dedicated Oscar Mayer wienermeister that I was, kept our shop open for the hard-core afternoon beer drinkers who would drop by and knock one out before heading home. Amy would stop in for a soft drink or a glass of water and maybe even an occasional hot dog (the vegetarian restaurant on the other side of the warehouse might have been healthier, but even Amy lives dangerously now and then). It was during those times, she now tells me, when Amy would be sitting on a stool at the hot dog stand, that she first grew to like country music—that was all I played on the radio back in my early, militant years. Maybe it was the smell of hot dogs and beer mixed with the sound of a steel guitar that snagged her. Whatever it was, Amy has since confided to me that if it weren't for the Saucy Dog stand, there might never have been a Bluebird Cafe. Though this definitely is something I would love to claim credit for, I think even if we had never met, one way or another Amy Kurland would have ended up founding the Bluebird Cafe. Every now and then some people are lucky enough to achieve their destiny. You can tell who they are by the dedication and love they put into their work. Amy is one of these people. Her commitment to songwriters and love of songs is obvious in the way she runs the Bluebird. In a town where songwriters are a nickel a dozen (yeah, the price has gone down lately), Amy treats every songwriter like a multiplatinum artist, demanding that they get the attention and respect they deserve when they perform at the Bluebird. That goes for not only the established hit makers but the fresh-off-the-freeway Sunday-night novices.

This is what makes the Bluebird what it is and always has been. And knowing that Amy Kurland gives me a small part of the credit for this landmark she has created makes me proud. But whenever I am sitting in the Bluebird witnessing one of those special moments that you will read about in this book, that is when I am most proud . . . to be a songwriter.

■   ■   ■   ■   ■

In addition to teaching Amy to dig country music, this Georgia native has been a longtime friend of T. Graham Brown and written several of his hits, including "The Last Resort."

The interior of the Green Hills Game Room, soon to be the Bluebird.

Much of the work of transforming the old game room into a new listening room was done by Amy and her friends, some of whom just happened to be musicians, no doubt excited about the prospect of a new venue in town. Soulshouter and British transplant Frank Sheen was among them. So were Roberto Bianco, Pebble Daniel, Ralph Vitello, and Mike Bonnell. Some musicians make better handymen than others, though.

Kevin Welch

For many years there was a loose, probably dangerous electrical outlet on the stage of the Bluebird. There are two outlets; this is the one

We're keeping Dustin Welch in the kitchen and away from AC outlets. His dad, Kevin, couldn't be prouder.

at stage left. Anyone who ever had to play on that side of the stage with anything to plug in during those years will remember this. It had detached from the wall and just dangled by the wires, and every time you had to plug your amp or whatever into it, you had to wonder when the sparks were gonna start flying. It literally stayed like that for, I don't know, five years? I cussed it just like everyone else until finally Amy had someone fix it. What I have never told anyone is that way back

when the interior of the Bluebird was being built, I had stopped in to see what was happening. I was told that this was to be a new place to play, and in those days music venues for guys like me were pretty rare. So in the spirit of helping the cause, I jumped right in and did a little work that day. The one job I actually did was to install the stage-left A.C. outlet. So, there you have it. I confess. It was all my fault. Sorry, y'all.

▪ ▪ ▪ ▪ ▪

Like fine wine, Kevin Welch just gets better with time. He did his stint as a Music Row writer, but it wasn't until he released his own music that his true talents were realized. Western Beat, Life Down Here on Earth, *and* Beneath My Wheels *contain some of the finest folk/country songs you'll ever hear.*

It's hard to believe Kevin Welch ever had hair this short … and that it was attached to Vince Gill.

Roy S. Hatcher, Former Davidson County District Fire Chief

Amy, this is a little trivia about the first day that you opened the cafe. Do you remember what happened? Well, you blew all the fuses in your fuse box and created a scare. The Fire Department responded and found your trouble, and then we all started talking. You were the most excited girl I have ever seen. You told how your father was helping you get started and that you hoped it was a big success, which it has been. You contacted an electrician to come out and fix the deal. I was the district chief who responded. I stayed around for a little while and talked and tried to assure you that everything would be all right and that you would be a success. You said that you would offer me a cup of coffee

Shiny, happy people. Here's one of our earliest crews. Left to right: Lisa Taylor, Amy, Michael Perkins, Jackie Welch, Martha Bickley, and Mark Benner.

but you couldn't make any until you got your trouble fixed. I said that was okay but I would let you owe me one. I would come back later and get my coffee. Well, to make a long story short, I never did. I retired in 1985, and I am now seventy-eight years old and have followed your success through the news. I just want you to know that I'm proud of you

19

and I'm glad you blew your fuse on the first day or I would never have met you. I still pass your place every few days. I just thought I would bring back some memories to you. Hope you continue to have great success.

■　■　■　■　■

(Amy's managed to keep the power on—for the most part—and still wants to make good on that cup of coffee for Roy.)

All the bugs were finally worked out, and the club opened with Jay Patten and his band playing the first notes.

Another pic from the early days. That's Jay Patten blowing the sax, Robert Bianco on the mic, and Toni Sehulster on the bass.

Foster & Lloyd were among the first acts to hone their chops and launch their careers at the Bluebird.

Jay Patten

I've got a trunk full of Bluebird Cafe memories that reach way back to before the opening night, June 14, 1982 . . . back to when the nicest little showcase nightclub in the whole wide world was just a gleam of an idea in Amy Kurland's smile. Of all the wonderful things that have happened to me through music, I'm most proud to be able to say that I, along with a marvelous band, was the first performer to set foot on that magical little stage. Since then I've had the honor of hosting the Bluebird anniversary and Christmas shows (at this writing we're preparing for the seventeenth anniversary show).

Back to opening night. I remember standing onstage and admiring the audience. They were beautiful. The room was a big smile from nine-thirty to the wee small hours. People could feel that something was going on. From the very first downbeat there was something special about the Bluebird.

After thirty years of being on the

road, performing in some of the best concert halls (Lincoln Center, Royal Festival Hall, et cetera), and working some of the most happening clubs (New York, L.A., London, Vegas), I can honestly say that performing on the stage of the Bluebird Cafe with the likes of Jimmy Hall, Jonell Mosser, Crystal Gayle, John Prine, T. Graham Brown, Rita Coolidge, Vince Gill, Michael Johnson, Ashley Cleveland, Vickie Carrico, Tracy Nelson, Roberto Bianco, and so many more has been the most satisfying and lucky experience a sax player from Jersey could ever have.

How time flies. Here are the boys nearly twenty years later.

■ ■ ■ ■ ■

In between Bluebird gigs, Jay Patten has released several albums of his unique brand of swing and jazz and continues to work as the musical director for Crystal Gayle's band.

Rita Coolidge was a very special guest at the 13th Anniversary Bash.

Bob Mater

Early on, the Bluebird was a band venue. It was known as a "listening room." No dancing, just bands and fans. Songwriter-mecca status was still a few years away, but the seeds were being sown. You could look out from the bandstand and see every face in the audience. They were listening. They were paying attention. As a club-date veteran, used to music often being no more than background accompaniment for a conversation, I found this a beautiful thing.

I know that these days the Bluebird has a trademark on the word *shhh*, but these folks were *strong*. We used to just peel the paint back on those gigs, and frankly I sometimes wonder how the audience took it. I remember one night with Vickie, ex–Elton John drummer Nigel Olsen was sitting right beside the bandstand. Now, here's a guy who has played his share of stadium concerts. Of course I was trying to impress him, flailing away mightily. After the set he came up to say hi, and he asked me, "Why are you playing so loud?" I was just so proud.

On the other end of the decibel universe was Mose Allison, the legendary blues/jazz singer and piano player who we used to back up when he came through town. One night he caught the sound guy miking the bass drum. Mose thought this was the funniest thing he had ever seen. He asked me, "Why would you want to mike a bass drum? It's plenty loud." Good question. I know the answer of course, but still a good question.

All good things come to an end, however, with the notable exception of the Bluebird Cafe, which has nourished and encouraged local talent for all these years, and continues to do exactly that. Thanks.

■   ■   ■   ■

Bob Mater is a drummer with a list of credits a mile long. He's also a longtime friend of Amy's and the Bluebird Cafe.

Roberto Bianco, the Romantic Voice of Our Time

I had been traveling around the world, spreading the musical message of love to countless diehard fans, when I received a code-a-phone message from my best friend, Bob White. Now, Bob and I have an unusual relationship in that you never see us together but you know that we are inseparable. In 1982 Amy Kurland and Bob had opened

Yes, here he is: "the Romantic Voice of Our Time," Roberto Bianco.

up the Bluebird Cafe and both were anxious for me to take time off from my busy schedule and come to Nashville and play at the grand opening. How could I refuse? A chance to sing romantic songs in Music City, USA! What a treat!

In the early days of '82, the population of Nashville was quite small. Small enough so that everyone could fit into the Bluebird. Now, of course, Nashville has become a metro area and some people are having to stand in line to even get into the Bluebird. Alas, though you may have to endure cramped conditions, it is always worth it because the music transcends all limitation.

Like myself, love and romance are ageless. The Bluebird Cafe, be-the talents of these writers. More important, I was inspired by their work, their love of what they were doing, and their readiness to encourage aspiring writers.

The Bluebird had become very much a home for me, filled with people who cared about one another. It was and still is a wonderful place to sit and listen to someone's unique take on life or love. There was never a night without a song that amazed and inspired you. A strong common thread between the hacks and the pros was the genuine love of a well-placed word or a melody that followed you out into the cold Nashville-winter night.

I went to the Bluebird alone to celebrate my thirtieth birthday only to find Marshall Chapman's, uh, thirty-second birthday party in full swing, and was invited to be a part of that. That first Bluebird year was for me a year of magical nights where I soaked up fine songwriting, superb musicianship, and great good humor, and I made lifelong friends. It was a very tangible place for the craft of songwriting. When someone asks me about writing songs, I think of those times and try to give helpful advice and encouragement. The Bluebird Cafe's influence on music is not to be underestimated, and I will always be glad that I was there, if only for a time. I know that it will always be a part of who I am as an entertainer, musician, and writer. I left town in 1988 and spent twelve years in the Caribbean as the resident entertainer at the Hyatt Regency Grand Cayman. I have recently returned to the States, and find myself crisscrossing the country. Every time I come through Nashville, the *very first place* I go to is the Bluebird Cafe. To me it's a physical reminder of why I do what I do, and just being there is to take a long cool drink from the well of inspiration. See you on your thirtieth birthday! Here is a song I wrote back then, inspired by, well, you know . . .

Bluebird

I guess there was some luck involved, but I did search
   high and low
Looking for a special song that no one else would know
Then I heard the Bluebird
Above the city's noise I heard an artist's melody
and like no other song I'd heard before it called to me
Sing softly, Bluebird
Oh, Bluebird, I've finally found a friend

cause of its focus on the singer-songwriter—the nucleus of all music—will be a constant enduring reminder that a great song will always be a great song, whether it be new or old.

The Bluebird Cafe is music, life, love, and romance, and I am so happy to be a part of it.

■　■　■　■　■

Roberto Bianco's smooth, sensuous song stylings are always the highlight of the Bluebird's Christmas and anniversary bashes. He's been a contributing columnist to Nashville's In Review *weekly and appeared in the movie* Ernest Goes to Camp.

James White

In the late summer of 1986 I was twenty-nine years old and had moved to Nashville after a backpacking trip to Europe. I had less than ten dollars to my name when I arrived and moved in with two of the four people that I knew in town. I had been in a band in California with those four, and we had immigrated to Nashville at different times and for different reasons. They all told me that I needed to get over to the Bluebird to hear great songwriters. That little place on Hillsboro Road was to become the focal point of my life for the next year and a half and my postgraduate school as a songwriter.

After I had found a part-time job working for RC Cola, I started going to the Bluebird. I auditioned to perform on Writers Night, made the cut, and evidently did a good enough job that after several appearances, Amy told me she was thinking of doing an early show and asked if I would be interested. So I was the first singer-songwriter to start the regular Early Show lineup. At the Bluebird I met other new writers and together we started a writers' group named for a pet fish in hopes that we would sound important when we were announced. We were the Hal Bass Group.

I often took the cover charge at the door. I helped repaint the place that year and helped decorate for the New Year's party of 1989. I had also begun to run the sound there and count myself lucky to have been behind the board for many of the legendary In the Round performances by writers like Schuyler, Knobloch, Schlitz, and Overstreet, and one of my heroes, John Prine. To be sure, I was somewhat in awe of

Oh, Bluebird, you know that I'll be back again to hear
Tomorrow's song today and watch the stars begin
   to rise
Oh, Bluebird, you were such a nice suprise
And there beneath your wings I learned that life can be
   a song
Melody and harmony and you and me belong together
Bluebird
I can sing my own words and know someone really cares
And maybe I'll fly higher than I ever thought I'd dare
Thanks to you, Bluebird
Oh, Bluebird, I've finally found a friend
Oh, Bluebird, you know that I'll be back again to hear
Tomorrow's song today and watch the stars begin
   to rise
Oh, Bluebird, you were such a nice suprise

■　　■　　■　　■　　■

James White has five CDs of original music. His song "Blame It On the Rum" appears in the movie The Firm.

John Manion

The other night I drove past the arena and the new Country Music Hall of Fame. I thought about how much Nashville has changed since I moved here in 1981, a clueless kid with a full head of hair and a waistline! I guess what I miss the most about the early eighties is the sense of musical community that existed back then.

It seemed like ground zero was the space between the bar and the bathroom at the Bluebird. That's where I met Ashley Cleveland, Pam Tillis, Vince Gill, Vickie Carrico, Larry Chaney, and Kevin Welch. Everyone was on the same page. Now, years later, some of us are world-famous and some of us are still waiting tables.

Here's the poster that was tacked to hundreds of utility poles around Nashville to announce the opening of a new club in Green Hills.

I guess what I miss most about the early years of the Bluebird, before the invasion of the Stetsons, was that the Bluebird was a testing ground and a watering hole combined. You could play your autobiographical, minor-key ditties, and people would say, "Hey, I can relate." We were all products of the Joni Mitchell/James Taylor school of songwriting.

The Sweethearts of the Rodeo made a name for themselves at the 'Bird. They got a record deal too.

But things change, and so indeed did the musical climate in Nashville. I remember always catching great showcases. I was at Kathy Mattea's earliest showcase. I was there when the Sweethearts of the Rodeo got their deal. I was blown away by Jill Sobule and consider her a friend and a major influence on my sound. I played a gig with the Indigo Girls before they got their deal. I did a successful "Johnny O'Manion" St. Paddy's Day benefit show at the Bluebird. I also did the first draft of my one-man show, *Total Picture*, at the 'Bird.

It was like being at school.

■　■　■　■　■

John Manion is a singer-songwriter originally from New Jersey. He's released three self-produced albums, I Am a Wave, Little Movies, *and* The Total Picture. *He describes his music as "folk Broadway."*

CHAPTER 2

THE EARLY YEARS

AUDITIONS, FIRST IMPRESSIONS & BIG DEALS

THE WAY WE WERE

Quick, grab a napkin. This could be a song.

Within the first month of opening its doors, the Bluebird Cafe was graced by a performance from Don Everly of the Everly Brothers. It definitely doesn't hurt to have a legend play your club in the first few weeks.

At the time, Amy was keeping the books and helping out in the kitchen. She had Hugh and Jewdy Bennett handling the bookings. Both the restaurant and the music club were getting rave reviews, but the music was probably get-

Roger Cook yucks it up with John Prine and Ron Davies.

ting the biggest buzz. Steve Earle, Tim Krekel, Roger Cook, Casey Kelly, and Angela Kaset all played the Bluebird that first year. With the closing of the old Exit/In, we were obviously filling a void by carrying on the tradition of regular Writers Nights.

Over the next few years the Bluebird Cafe solidified its reputation as the best showcase club in Nashville. The bookings were diverse. Rock, pop, folk, country, R & B, jazz, and blues were all part of the musical menu. We even had the occasional poetry reading and comedy act.

If you can't get a table you can usually get a seat in the pews. Hymnals are not provided.

It seems everyone remembers their first time at the Bluebird. Fortunately for us all, most of the memories are fond ones. People also love to talk about their favorite shows and the friendships that were begun in our little room.

Don Schlitz

Dear Amy,

Do you remember?

It happened a long, long time ago. You had a new club. You were booking bands and doing okay. One day we were talking in the parking lot and I was trying to convince you that people would pay to see songwriters play their own songs. You were skeptical, as a businesswoman, but you were intrigued as an artist in your own right. So you gave it a shot.

You lost a lot of money, but you never stopped trying. And it took a long, long time. But it worked. Amy, you made it work. Now the whole world considers the Bluebird Cafe to be the best songwriters' club ever. Period.

But do you want to know a secret? I didn't know if it would work or not.

I was just trying to get a gig.

Love, Don (4A$)

■　■　■　■　■

Don Schlitz is one of the most successful songwriters of the last twenty years. See the Don Schlitz sidebar on pages 31–32 for the complete story.

Jonell Mosser

The first time I remember coming into the Bluebird I sat down at the bar and saw one of the little embedded mother-of-pearl birds at the end of the bar and put my hand over it. I guess I wanted to hold it, it was so pretty. I saw Amy that night and could hardly believe that someone my age had it together enough to own such a cool place. Anyway, I don't remember who played that night—it was probably Jay Patten's old band. I do remember seeing Pebble Daniel and hearing one of the band members ask her to sit in when they came back from their break. We had to leave before she sang.

The next time I came back, Yo Mama (the all-girl band I was in) was booked there. During the sound check I watched Amy and was sure she was going to tell us to pack up and forget about the gig that night. I think our version of "Come On in My Kitchen" won her over. That night we were playing furiously for about seventy people (that was a crowd to us), and my friend Sharon, who was taking the door, asked me to repeat a song. I really didn't want to do it, but she convinced me it was important. It was an Aretha Franklin cover. Well, the two guys standing at the door all but carried me off the stage. They were from France and were recording an album for Johnny Halliday ("the Elvis of France") at Sound Emporium and were looking for, as they put it, "white girls who sound like black girls." So I got my first session.

■   ■   ■   ■   ■

Perhaps no other artist in the history of the Bluebird has garnered such a fervent and faithful fan base as Jonell Mosser. This Kentucky girl mixes the fire of Janis Joplin with the soul of Aretha Franklin.

Jonell Mosser radiates both onstage and off.

Michael Johnson

I have so many Bluebird memories that I don't know where to begin. Witnessing SKB in the early days, and watching the unbelievable wit, magic, and chemistry of that group. Or the night the power went out in a big storm and we did our In the Round by candlelight, to a rapt audience, who stayed the entire night—wonderful. And so many more.

The people I've met at the Bluebird over the years are legion: Roberto Bianco, Don Henry, Gary Burr, Jonell Mosser, Gene Nelson, W. T. Davidson, Mike Henderson, to name a few—and always the occasional drifter from L.A. or Ireland or somewhere, who sits in and blows your socks off.

Here's Michael Johnson with singer-songwriter Randy Van Warmer.

But the most endearing memory is of lunches there when I was working on my first real Nashville album. 1984. I was commuting from Minnesota then, staying in a cheap hotel. Despite previous visits and even pop-music success, I knew no one. I'd sit and do my homework there. I had recorded a song called "Give Me Wings," and just like most of the dreamers and wannabes who walked through that door, I was sure I was on to something.

With no reason to be so, everyone there was receptive, more than nice—giving loving encouragement and real understanding to a little lonely guy who sat there with his notebook, knowing, then wondering, then doubting, then knowing again that maybe there was room for him in this town. That to me is what the Bluebird has always been about. Amy, you will always have my heartfelt thanks.

■   ■   ■   ■   ■

Michael Johnson's career has spanned three decades. As a pop artist he's known best for "Bluer Than Blue" and "This Night Won't Last Forever." As a country artist he scored with "That's That," "The Moon Is Still Over Her Shoulder," and "Ponies." Most recently he penned the Forerunner hit "Cain's Blood."

Allen Shamblin is as nice as he is talented and that's saying a lot.

Allen Shamblin

When asked about my earliest memories at the Bluebird Cafe, I drift back to late 1989. I was only one year removed from slinging boxes in a warehouse, where I earned a hundred and fifty bucks a week. The arches of my feet are still hurting from working all day on that hard concrete in cheap tennis shoes. Around this time Don Schlitz invited me to open a show for him at the Bluebird. I both anticipated and dreaded the performance. I'd sung into a microphone fewer than a half a dozen times in my life—and then only with my eyes closed tight and my fingers trembling to the point that I'd stop trying to play chords on my guitar and just sing a cappella.

The big night arrived, and I performed a few songs to open Don's first set and a few more to open his second set. The whole experience reminded me of the time I *tried* to ride a bull growing up in Texas. Utter terror before the bucking started, and a total rush after the dust settled and I still had all my teeth and I wasn't wearing a full-body cast.

Don went on to play until around 1:30 A.M. He captivated the audience with at least two dozen "hits" mixed in with another dozen songs that I thought should have been hits or soon would be. Sweat streamed down his cheeks as he sang and told hilarious stories. He gave everything he had, and the audience, including myself, was blown away.

At the end of the evening I went up to Don and thanked him for the great opportunity he'd given me. Before I could walk away, he said, "Hey, wait a minute. You forgot something." Then he handed me three hundred dollars, which was exactly half of what he made that night. I said, "No way," because the people had paid to see him, not me, and besides, I'd only played a handful of

DON SCHLITZ

Don Schlitz came to Nashville from Durham, North Carolina. The year was 1973, and Don was all of twenty years old. His first job in Music City was working as a computer operator at Vanderbilt University. He opted for the graveyard shift so he could write and pitch his songs during the day.

It's rare that a songwriter's very first cut goes on to become a Grammy winner and is named CMA Song of the Year, but that's just what happened to Don in 1978 when Kenny Rogers recorded "The Gambler." It would be several years before he'd see that kind of success again.

From the earliest days of the Bluebird, Don has been with us. It's hard to believe, but back then he'd play to nobody. The waitresses and bartender would sit at tables to give him an audience to play to. A few years later he had his next big hit, "Stand a Little Rain," recorded by the Nitty Gritty Dirt Band. As the eighties moved forward, Don would begin to see his songs recorded by John Conlee, Alabama, Michael Johnson, the Judds, and Randy Travis. Travis's recording of "Forever and Ever, Amen" was Don's second Grammy-winning song and was also named Song of the Year by the CMA. It was just one of many songs cowritten with Paul Overstreet, one of Don's most successful collaborators.

As Don continued to write one chart-topping song after another, he was named ASCAP's Songwriter of the Year for four consecutive years, 1988–1991, and was inducted into the Nashville Songwriters Association Hall of Fame in 1993.

It was right here at the Bluebird that Don met his wife, Polly. The story goes that it was love at first sight, the room ceased to exist, it was just the

(continued)

songs. But Don would hear nothing of it. And the truth is I guess he knew I could use the money. Over the next couple of years I opened shows for Don almost once a month at the Bluebird. I'd have done it for free, but he always paid me half the door. That's what I'll always remember about my early days at the Bluebird Cafe.

．　．　．　．　．

Ask songwriters to name a song they wish they'd written, and many would list the Bonnie Raitt classic "I Can't Make You Love Me." Well, Allen Shamblin did write it, and it's just one of many great songs this man from Texas has penned. Others include "I Thought He Walked on Water," "Thinkin' Problem," and "In This Life."

DON SCHLITZ

two of them. They're still together today. (Heavy sigh.)

Don was the man who introduced us to the Sweethearts of the Rodeo and Baillie and the Boys. Both acts would become Bluebird favorites and launch their careers from our stage. They were just two of many acts that Don brought in as part of his "Don and His So-Called Friends" shows. Once he started playing with Fred Knobloch, Thom Schuyler, and Paul Overstreet, however, history was truly made. On stage, In the Round, at the bar, they've played in every configuration imaginable and always made it fun.

The latest Don Schlitz institution has been the "Don for a Dollar" shows. He'd asked Amy what she thought people would pay to see him play solo. She suggested ten or twelve bucks. Don thought it ought to be a buck. And so it was—and is to this day. Many of the shows were recorded, and a CD was released with all proceeds benefitting the St. Patrick's Homeless Shelter. Thousands of dollars were raised. Unfortunately, the *Don for a Dollar* CD is now out of print, making it a collector's item.

Don Schlitz and the Bluebird have been musical mates for nearly twenty years. We look forward to the next twenty.

Other Don Schlitz hits include

"Give Me Wings"
"I Won't Take Less Than Your Love"
"Strong Enough to Bend"
"I Feel Lucky"
"The Old School"
"He Thinks He'll Keep Her"
"I Think About You"
"The Greatest"

Josh Leo

Radio City Music Hall, the Filmores East and West, the Whisky à Go Go, and the Troubadour Club. All sacred houses and the most holy of musical institutions. Why would one dare to include the Bluebird in the list? A very small, dark, and unlikely club, in a bad strip mall in Green Hills. But on many a night to the few who are lucky enough to be packed like sardines into this tiny club, the Bluebird is transformed into a sacred shrine. I have been one of the fortunate sons many a night, standing up on the one-foot-tall stage, feeling like some sort of musical giant.

But the one night I'll never forget was when the Del Beatles, a copy band full of session musicians, writers, and producers, played a fiftieth-birthday party for the late Dale Franklin. Dale, to anyone who was priviledged to meet her, was an innovative leader in the musical community, and a true spirit. From the moment of the countoff into the first song to the thunderous crashing of the last note, the place was electric! Everyone in the club was floating about six inches off the ground and didn't even notice. That night there were no thoughts of yesterday, no worries of tomorrow, no deadlines to meet, people to see, careers to start, or bills to pay—just the now. That night time did actually stand still.

Josh Leo tears it up with the Del Beatles.

It was the most alive I think I have ever been. Who would have thought it would have happened at the Bluebird! I miss you, Dale.

■   ■   ■   ■   ■

Josh Leo is a hit songwriter, producer, and session guitarist and was formerly the vice president of A & R at RCA Records. His hits include "Sittin' on Go," recorded by Paul Brandt. A devoted hockey fan, he plays in a part-time band made up of members of the Nashville Predators hockey team.

Not everyone has a completely pleasant first-time-at-the-Bluebird memory, however. Many artists and writers came through the door and had their hats handed to them as they realized they were not quite the caliber they wanted to be—yet.

Janis Ian

I'd hit the tarmac at the old Nashville airport in March 1986 and immediately felt at home. In fact, I immediately wanted to move to Nashville. The first time I went to the Bluebird was my first week in town, when someone invited me to go see SKO. I remember it vividly because Thom Schuyler, Fred Knobloch, and Paul Overstreet completely blew me away. On top of that, Don Schlitz was playing, and the qual-

Janis Ian has been a friend of Amy's and the Bluebird since her arrival in Nashville. She's even helped us judge the auditions.

ity of songwriting was so high that I decided then and there to go into another profession. I was completely depressed for days. It

33

seemed like everywhere I went, people played better, wrote better, and sang better than I did. Even the hotel staff were songwriters (I discovered that while trying to pick up my messages one night; I had to wait until they finished the bridge).

The Bluebird became my haven, and remained so for a long time. I moved to Nashville flat broke, living in a furnished rental apartment above a parking lot. I had no money for entertainment, no money for cable, no money for eating out. Instead, I went to the Bluebird three or four nights a week, getting there in time for the earliest show and nursing my beer until closing. I got a serious education, became friendly with the waitresses, and even faced the dreaded Amy in her lair. It was a place I could go when I knew no one in town, where people were tolerant of my "northernness" and friendly enough that I always felt welcome. I miss those days.

■　■　■　■　■

Janis Ian was a pop phenomenon while still a teenager. Her first single, "Society's Child," was as popular as it was controversial. "At Seventeen" won her a Grammy, and "Jesse" has been recorded by Roberta Flack and Joan Baez.

Marc Beeson

About two weeks after I moved to Nashville, in August 1990, I went to the Bluebird for the first time. In the Round that night were

Mike Reid, Gary Burr, Beth Nielsen Chapman, and Eric Kaz. It was an important moment for me because I realized I had set a certain watermark for my writing. Suddenly, that watermark was much higher, and it was a serious wake-up call. I had been scraping around at capillary depth, while these people were reaching for the arteries. I've been digging ever since.

*Marc Beeson looks like he has mischief on his mind.
That or more hits.*

■　■　■　■　■

Marc Beeson had one of country's biggest crossover hits with the Restless Heart smash "When She Cries." He's also penned hits like "Even Now, I Wouldn't Know" and "Phones Are Ringing All Over Town."

AUDITIONS

Picturing Your Audience in Their Undies

For more than a few writers, their first memories of the Bluebird are the dreaded auditions (Bom-bom-bom-bom). For "less developed" writers, standing up in front of an audience of peers as well as AMY, could send them into a catatonic state. Over the years we've seen a few brave souls simply stop and walk off the stage—it was just too much for them. Of course, we've also experienced some "performers" who probably never should have stepped on the stage in the first place. Oh, well. The auditions are always a slightly perverse pleasure, a veritable cattle call of dreamers laying it all on the line with a verse and chorus of their best song. We just don't have them as often as we used to.

In the early days, auditions were held every Sunday afternoon, with the best of the crop performing that evening in a writers' show-case. We were fashioning our system after the Exit/In's old process, with Gail Terry handling it all. As the popularity of the Writers Night grew, we were forced to cut back auditions to once a month. We were seeing more good writers than we had room for. As many as a hundred and fifty have auditioned for a Sunday-night slot. Eventually, we had to reduce auditions to once a quarter. Even then, auditioners could expect to wait six to eight months for their scheduled Writers Night—should they pass their audition.

And still they come. From every corner of the country they come, with a dream in their hearts and a song on their lips. It's almost spiritual.

Marcus Hummon

In my first week in Nashville, back in 1986, I too made my "haj," my pilgrimage to the Bluebird Cafe for the Sunday Writers Night. I auditioned for none other than Amy herself and was very pleased to be scheduled to come back.

Nashville being the congenial city it is, I had already met a number of people in town, and several had come out to see me. When my turn came up, I gave a nervous and at times frenetic little set. The crowd seemed to be into it, and I was very pleased with myself, certain that in no time I'd be at the top—or something like that.

Well, several other pilgrims from all over the land of Oz tried their craft out on the audience, as I listened and received accolades from new friends. Then all of a sudden, it was time for the special guest writer, Kevin Welch.

Marcus Hummon explains the fine art of songwriting and headwear.

I was unaware that this was part of the drill, so I perked up my ears to see what this long-haired, drowsy Oklahoma boy could do. He stood up there and played one song after another, each making me sick to my stomach, and by the time he got to Moe Bandy's hit, "Too Old to Die Young," I wanted to throw up. . . . You see, the songs were so wonderful, the characters so much more alive and full than mine, and I had this sinking feeling that a pilgrim gets when he knows how long the road lies ahead before some destination, or when some mirage dissipates, and the hot, dry facts remain.

Three years later I had my first cut, and single: Michael Martin Murphey's "Pilgrims on the Way."

■   ■   ■   ■   ■

A child of missionary parents, Marcus Hummon can call the world his hometown. As a songwriter, he brings fresh perspective and direction to country radio with hits like "Only Love," "One of These Days, Ready to Run," "Cowboy Take Me Away," and "The Cheap Seats."

Mark Luna

I have countless memories of the Bluebird. Many are of my own performances, even more are from other writers and artists. The one memory that will forever stay with me was my audition for the Sunday-night show, my first performance there ever.

Janis Ian was there, along with Amy. Midway through my very first song (a Dan Fogelberg album cut, no less) the mike (boom) stand began to descend. I watched in horror. Half the room started laughing (along with Janis and Amy), and the other half (mostly auditioners) panicked. When the stand fell below the point of no return, I stood up tall and sang as *loud* as I could, sweat streaming down my "why me?" face. I passed. And the rest is history.

■ ■ ■ ■ ■

With his good looks and soaring tenor, Mark Luna has become a very popular Bluebird regular, especially among our female customers. As a songwriter he's a definite favorite of Lee Roy Parnell, who had a big hit with Luna's "When a Woman Loves a Man."

MORE STRANGE EXPERIENCES

I Always Do That Onstage

Roger Cook

Way back, probably in the first year of the Bluebird, I was doing a spot with my ukelele and sitting in the front row was none other than Francis Preston [BMI president]. She seemed to be really enjoying the performance and smiling a bunch, and it wasn't until after the show that she confessed that her amusement was caused by the fact that my family jewels were on display, peeking from the corner of my very tight shorts. She's never forgotten it, and neither have I.

■ ■ ■ ■ ■

Roger Cook is a native of England. His biggest claim to fame is as cowriter of the world-famous anthem "I'd Like to Teach the World to Sing." He's not resting on past successes, however. Since arriving in Nashville he's penned the huge George Strait single "I Just Want to Dance with You."

Roger Cook, keeping things together with John Prine.

Fred Knobloch

First gig. Having played at the Bluebird Cafe once at a showcase for the Nashville office of CBS/Columbia Records, which distributed Scotti Bros. records, my label at the time, I thought that when I moved to town I could pick up some easy money playing there.

I was in the process of leaving Scotti Bros. and was having trouble making ends meet, so sometime in the spring of '83 I cajoled Amy into getting me a night by myself. Now, bear in mind that I was not that good a writer (some say I'm still not) and was basically going to do a seventy-five-minute club show, say "Thank you," and get out with a few coins in my pocket. Suffice it to say, there was not going to be a lot of great original songwriting going on.

The always shy and reserved Fred Knobloch makes a point.

Show time came, and remarkably, none of the 176 people who bought my solo album (released in 1981) were there. In fact, of the almost five and a half billion people in the world at the time, only about thirty-five braved the elements and made it out for my "official" Music City debut. And what happened in the first three minutes onstage made them the darkest moments of my professional career.

To begin with, I was so nervous you could pop corn on my right hand. Flop sweat was streaming from the crown of my head, and to make matters worse, my G-string peg sagged right after "Ladies and gentlemen, Fred Knobloch" (polite smattering of what would graciously be called applause), so I began my first number more than slightly out of tune.

Then I did something you should never do, which is stop to retune. Next thing I know, my brand-new acoustic guitar system began to make a hissing noise, followed by a kind of wrinkled-paper effect that, with the reverb, produced a sound somewhat like a tin can sliding across a subway platform. All in a flash, I began career-reassessment training right on the stage of the Bluebird Cafe. A puff of blue smoke rose out of the back of my Roland Space Echo, and the guitar went dead. I mumbled something or other into the microphone and quickly began rerigging my guitar to play acoustically on an open mike. After about a minute (the first accurate measurement of eternity in history), I was back to the mike and ready to go.

Commencing the first number, which right now I believe was "Fishin' Blues" by Taj Mahal, I seemed to have it all working well when the vocal mike, which was on a boom stand, ever so slowly began to fall. Of course, being the consummate professional, I began to follow it down . . . down . . . down . . . until it thunked on the face of my guitar. At which point I continued playing as if it were an instrumental and stepped back out of the way. Along with the rest of the audience, I continued to follow the mike's progress downward until it pointed squarely at the stage monitor and let out a feedback squeal of immense proportions. The crowd (I use the term loosely) was squirming as if they were watching the last three minutes of *I Love Lucy* waiting for the other shoe to drop. I can only recall how far away the door was.

But I collected myself, picked up the mike, and screwed that boom on so tightly that even to this day no one can set that mike stand to any other position. It is still in the closet at stage right and may be viewed by one and all. I remember where I stood on the stage that night, and I have never again stood on that exact spot lest I go tumbling once more down the black hole of the Bluebird Cafe.

■　■　■　■

Fred Knobloch can best be described as a renaissance man. He's a writer's writer and a killer guitarist, and he wails like the Mississippi soul man he is. He hit the charts as a solo artist in the eighties with "Why Not Me?" and later as a member of SKB with the number-one hit "Baby's Got a New Baby." George Strait, Lorrie Morgan, Kenny Rogers, John Anderson, and Trisha Yearwood have all covered Knobloch's tunes.

BIG DEALS IN A LITTLE ROOM

Or, Waiting for Our Percentages

Kathy Mattea was the first artist to launch her career at the Bluebird. She played at the club often during our first year and later that year signed a record deal with Mercury. Soon afterward, *Good Morning America* was in town looking to film a young country upstart. They chose Kathy, and she chose to be filmed at the Bluebird, thus giving her—and us—instant national exposure. From that point on, the Bluebird Cafe was THE PLACE to play.

We like to think we've helped several other artists reach that brass ring. They like to think so too.

Kathy Mattea

I had been playing Writers Nights and performers' nights there since the place opened in the early eighties and was thinking about trying to front a band for the first time in my life. I mentioned this to Jewdy,

Kathy Mattea cozies up with hubby, Jon Vezner, as Paul Williams listens.

who at the time was booking the schedule there. She immediately replied with "You need to do this, Kathy. It's the next step for you. How about January 27?" I was flabbergasted. I had thought of it as a kind of vague goal lurking out there in my foggy future somewhere. Now I had to come up with the songs and the band and figure the whole thing out.

So on January 27, 1983, I showed up for the gig—and couldn't find a parking place. There was a crowd outside the door, and we had to run our whole show twice in order to fit everybody in. It took me till about 4 A.M. to "come down." I decided to play there once a month, and by the time March rolled around, there were record executives from my new label, Mercury, in the front row. It was an amazing time.

And then there was the *Good Morning America* taping during Fan Fair of that year, when we dragged all the cameras and lights in during a Writers Night so they could film a segment on someone who had just recently gotten a record deal. . . . I remember my hairdresser had just given me the worst haircut of my life two days before.

■　　■　　■　　■　　■

This West Virginia native has been keeping country music real and vital for well over a decade. Songwriters in Nashville know Kathy Mattea as an artist willing to take chances, push boundaries, and record the songs other artists might not.

T. Graham Brown

I played the Bluebird maybe the third showcase I ever did, where it was just me and my band, and it was really the first time I had gotten my act totally together. I was so scared. I had played a showcase at the World's End, and then I played a showcase at Bogey's in Lion's Head Village, but something wasn't right and I couldn't put my finger on it. My publisher, Waylon Holyfield, and I went over to Dalt's, where we ran into Harlan Howard, and we were sitting around talkin' and drinkin' and I told them something was wrong but I didn't know what. They said, "Man, you're talking too much. You ought to be play-

T. Graham Brown. Great voice ... questionable shirt.

ing several songs and then talk a little and then play some more songs." So when I played the Bluebird my next show, I was conscious of that. It worked and I thought, "Now I've learned a new trick."

Also it was the mood in the place. The mood was so awesome—it was such a lovin' thing. There are three places in town—the Ryman, the Grand Ole Opry, and the Bluebird—where I try to sing my best, you know, I feel like those are the places where I can't disappoint. It's in my mind, I want to hit every note. I want to phrase it just right, and if I don't, it's like, "Dang, I did it at the Bluebird, I did it at the Bluebird." I don't feel like that anywhere else in town.

Amy, you've got a great thing over there at the Bluebird, and it's been great the way you've nurtured the songwriters and people too.

·   ·   ·   ·   ·

In the early nineties T. Graham Brown injected country music with a shot of soul and rhythm and blues. Hits like "Hell and High Water," "Come As You Were," and "Brilliant Conversationalist" made him a mainstay on both radio and video outlets. His most recent hit is the award-winning ballad "Wine into Water."

Trisha Yearwood

I've always thought the Bluebird was a magical place. Everyone walks in the door with dreams of being discovered or of seeing stars. I was no different. I met Kathy Mattea at the Bluebird. Wow. I got to see Don Schlitz perform at the Bluebird. Wow. For a newcomer to Nashville, to actually see the people who were writing and making the music that I loved and wanted so badly to be a part of was a dream come true. It was one of the things that inspired me to get off my *** and make it happen for myself.

Right after I signed with MCA Records in 1990, I had to do a showcase for the entire record label, of songs from the first album. I had never met half of these people, and of course I was terrified. I would be doing my show at the famous Bluebird, which made me even more nervous. I remember sound check in that empty room and

Trisha Yearwood with songwriter Jude Johnstone. Jude wrote the title track for Trisha's album Hearts in Armor.

knew that the nervousness I felt with no one there would only be magnified by ten by the time the place filled up that evening. I had bought a pair of black leggings and a gold jacket for the occasion. I remember that I had gone to a cloth store and bought a shiny button for the coat to replace the ordinary-looking one that it had so that I would look more like an "artist"!

The night ended up being magical and memorable, and the beginning of a wonderful career and a wonderful friendship with the Bluebird. It is one of the historic sites in Music City for me and for all. I'll bet someone is stepping through that door tonight, with that nervous anticipation of wondering who they'll spot or, even better, who they might meet. The dream goes on. I'm proud to be a part of it all.

■   ■   ■   ■   ■

Starting with "She's in Love with the Boy," Trisha Yearwood has compiled a list of hits to rival virtually anyone else in country music. "How Do I Live," "The Song Remembers When," "Wrong Side of Memphis," "In Another's Eyes," "The Woman Before Me," "Believe Me Baby (I Lied)" . . . the list goes on and on.

Faith Hill

Before getting my record deal, I spent the majority of my time at the Bluebird Cafe singing with Gary Burr. It was always a great treat to see my favorite songwriters in that particular environment. Gary was especially at his best when performing there. Martha Sharp [former senior vice president of A & R for Warner Bros.] first heard me sing at the Bluebird, and she subsequently signed me to Warner Bros. Records.

■　■　■　■　■

Since first hitting the charts with "Wild One," Faith Hill has been one of country's

Yep, that's Faith Hill, a year or two before she hit it big with "Wild One," lending her vocals to songwriter extraordinaire Gary Burr.

most consistent hit makers. Songs like "This Kiss" and "Breathe" have expanded her audience to include pop-music lovers. She's now considered one of pop's newest divas.

Bob DiPiero

I played many shows in the early days of the Bluebird as guitarist for John Scott Sherrill and the Wolves in Cheap Clothing. Scott loved to involve the crowd. We once had a contest where we gave away a very sick '68 Chevy Impala. All you had to do was guess how many empty beer cans were in the backseat. (There were hundreds.)

One of the most memorable nights at the Bluebird happened to be with the Wolves in Cheap Clothing. Dennis Robbins, John Scott, and I had been doing a lot of writing together, so we invited Dennis to the Bluebird to sit in with us and play some of these new songs. The contest that night slips my mind, but the winners got to be escorted to the nearest gas station, where the whole band would fill their car with gas, check the oil and the tires, wash the windshield, and buy them (a young, slightly starry-eyed couple) each a Moon Pie and an RC cola.

Bob DiPiero and members of Billy Hill, then known as Wolves in Cheap Clothing, make good on their offer to service the vehicle of one lucky member of the Bluebird crowd.

Much drinking was done on a Wolves gig. Usually what we made at the door just about covered our bar tab. Then there was the illicit activity going on out in the parking lot during the breaks. Needless to say, we rocked into the night getting

43

louder and drunker and higher and just having the best time you could possibly have with your clothes on.

Dennis Robbins brought his North Carolina Southern-rock groove to the gig, and the Wolves were going where no man had dared to go before. Actually, we were pretty oblivious to the crowd. Make that just pretty oblivious. There were wives there, ex-wives, future wives, future ex-wives, and assorted girlfriends.

We finally stopped playing at around 1:30 or 2 A.M. We stopped because the lovely Amy Kurland, Bluebird owner, threatened us in a so-very-creative but effective way. We stumbled over to the gas station with our contest winners and half the crowd from the 'Bird and fulfilled our contest promise.

The next morning, or should I say afternoon, I awoke to that dreaded ringing telephone. It was John Scott calling to tell me that there had been someone from Warner Bros. Records in the audience that night. We were offered a record deal, and we weren't even trying!

So with Dennis Robbins in tow, the Wolves in Cheap Clothing became Warner Reprise recording artists Billy Hill.

Bob DiPiero gets congratulated by Woody Bomar, head of Little Big Town Music, and Amy for being named Songwriter of the Year.

■   ■   ■   ■   ■

Bob DiPiero was named Songwriter of the Year at the 1998 Nashville Music Awards. He's received the CMA Triple Play Award for three number-one songs in one year: "Wink," "Take Me As I Am," and "Til You Love Me." This native of Youngstown, Ohio, was recently elected to the CMA board of directors.

John Scott Sherrill

Even though I have spent many wonderful years playing the Bluebird's In the Round Writers Nights, I can't help but remember those gigs in the early eighties with my band, the Wolves in Cheap Clothing. We were the motleyest of crews, and the club had not yet gained its international reputation as a listening room, so we were free to turn it up, especially when Dale Sellers would sit in with *stereo* twin reverb amps cranked to 9 on either side of the little stage. In those days it would get so wild I would be subject to involuntary falling down—a la James Brown—at the end of some shows. Martin Parker, Reno Kling, or Kevin Welch, not having a cape available, would toss a jacket over me and lead me gently backstage, where I would recover and bounce back to finish the song. In subsequent years I have tried, and will continue to try, to tone it down.

■　■　■　■　■

John Scott Sherrill has a way with words. As a member of Billy Hill and as a songwriter, he makes tunes that always hit the nail on the head—and the top of the charts. "Too Much Month at the End of the Money," "Nothin' but the Wheel," "How Long Gone," and "Some Fools Never Learn" are some of Sherrill's finest.

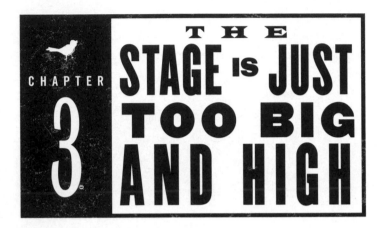

CHAPTER 3.

THE STAGE IS JUST TOO BIG AND HIGH

THE BIRTH OF IN THE ROUND

It kind of reminds you of the joke. **Q:** What's a redneck's last words? **A:** Hey, bubba! Watch this!

Rumor has it, Fred Knobloch and Don Schlitz *had* been drinking on the Sunday night they came into the cafe and offered up the following idea:

"Let's put four chairs in the middle of the room, facing each other, turn around the lights, and see what happens."

Thus, in 1985, the In the Round format was born at the Bluebird Cafe. It seemed like a crazy idea at the time, but now it's the most popular format at the club. In fact, In the Round and the Bluebird have become almost synonymous. While other clubs in Nashville and around the country have adopted the idea, none have matched the intimacy and magic that happens each time we put four chairs in the middle of the room.

Thom Schuyler

I recollect that the Greeks and the Romans first conceived and perfected the notion of a performance in the round. Several thousand years later, in 1985, to be exact, my friends Fred "Apollo" Knobloch and Don "Augustus" Schlitz came to the sober conclusion that this style of presentation needed to be resurrected in Nashville, the Athens of the South. The following Friday night at 9:30 P.M. I found myself sitting in a chair in the middle of the floor of the Bluebird Cafe with a microphone in front of me, facing south, looking directly at Paul Overstreet, who was staring directly back at me, while Don sat to my right and Fred to my left. We were about to embark on a strange, dramatic, and very funny musical journey, one that continues to this day.

SKB, otherwise known as Schuyler, Knobloch, and Bickhardt, doing what they do best.

The idea of several songwriters sitting around in a circle singing their songs and telling the stories of how and why those songs came to be is, to me at least, a hideous one. The setting is ripe with opportunity for indulgence, false sentiment, wimpy anecdotes, humiliation, vulgar pathos, drunken displays of sour grapes, and really bad music performed by songwriters who really wanted to be artists but couldn't sing or play all that well. I have witnessed and participated in enough of these ". . . and then I wrote" parades to testify to the fact that my assessment has some merit. However, this has all been overshadowed because I have had the great pleasure and good fortune to sit in that circle, almost exclusively, with Fred and Don. Their talent, humor, reliability, resilience, spontaneity, and sense of respect for those wonderful people who continue (fifteen years later) to come and see us do this

47

bit of un-show business has made the whole experience a watershed in my life.

So, the rebirth of the circular audience has now found its way around the world, again. Amy Kurland has sent In the Round missionaries to festivals, conferences, gatherings, and Wal-Mart openings from Quebec to Japan. They've been created for presidents, religious leaders, huge corporations, elementary schools, and Cub Scout fundraisers. The VH1 "Unplugged" series is traced directly to this little, 120-seat club in Green Hills. The format is utilized all over Los Angeles and London.

New York City's infamous "Words and Music" series at the Uptown Y even borrows from it. We re-created our living rooms, drank for free, and charged people five bucks to watch us have a great time. It's all Greek to me.

■　■　■　■　■

Thom Schuyler is one of the "big four," the original writers In the Round. Along with Craig Bickhardt and Fred Knobloch, he formed SKB and hit the charts with "This Old House" and "Baby's Got a New Baby." Other Schuyler hits include "Old Yellow Car" and "Sixteenth Avenue."

Craig Bickhardt

Thom Schuyler, Fred Knobloch, and Don Schlitz had come up with a new way of performing at the club. They had tried it a few times with Paul Overstreet, but Paul wasn't really into the idea. So they invited me to join them in an informal "in-the-round" setting where we all sat facing each other in the middle of the audience and swapped songs and stories for a few hours. At that time I don't think any of us really knew how perfectly this combination would fit into the Bluebird's intimate atmosphere.

We were already close friends, and the natural chemistry made the place feel like our living room. We knew just enough about each other's songs to throw a harmony or strum a few chords in the background. As the evening unfolded, the magic was obvious to everyone in the room. Every song seemed to inspire a performance better than the last. The unpolished harmonies and guitar parts reminded me of the first time I listened to the Band's *Big Pink* album.

At night's end we knew it was the beginning of something special.

Though we continued to perform In the Round for several years, for me nothing can top the high of that first show.

■　■　■　■　■

Craig Bickhardt replaced Paul Overstreet in our first and most famous In the Round foursome. His songs are a mix of musical innovation and lyrical inspiration. They include "Where I Used to Have a Heart," "In Between Dances," "I Can't Turn the Tide," and "You're the Power."

Paul Overstreet

I remember playing with Thom Schuyler, Fred Knobloch, and Don Schlitz. Singing songs like "On the Other Hand" and "One Love at a Time" and "Diggin' Up Bones" still looking for an artist to record them or lookin' for a record deal ourselves. In the audience one night was Tanya Tucker, who was a friend of Paul Davis. She later recorded "One Love at a Time" and several others. We had industry professionals there pitching "On the Other Hand" to George Jones and Merle Haggard. We didn't realize then

Paul Overstreet trades songs with his pal Paul Davis.

how many of these songs would later be number one records. Great times.

■　■　■　■　■

Paul Overstreet was a part of our first In the Round along with Schuyler, Knobloch, and Schlitz. He found it wasn't his thing, however, and decided to concentrate on his own solo career and cranking out hits like "Forever and Ever Amen," "On the Other Hand," "Long Line of Love," and many more.

ANYTHING MEN CAN DO . . .

The Creation of Women in the Round

Blame it on estrogen and that competitive spirit it brings out. Whatever the reason (equality?), Tricia Walker thought that perhaps there should be another In the Round playing at the Bluebird besides Schuyler, Knobloch, Schlitz, and Overstreet.

Tricia Walker

It wasn't long after the In the Round concept started in the mid-eighties with the great Don Schlitz, Fred Knobloch, Thom Schuyler, and Paul Overstreet that I wanted to see if I could find four women who could do an ITR just as good, if not better, than the guys.

After one (and only one) rehearsal, Ashley Cleveland, Pam Tillis,

The Women in the Round: Ashley Cleveland, Tricia Walker, Pam Tillis, and Karen Staley, showing off their fashion expertise.

Karen Staley, and I made our debut as the original Women in the Round in November 1988. I even have the tape. (Anybody interested in a little bootlegging?) Over the next ten years we played regularly at the Bluebird Cafe and came to be in pretty high demand. (Lord knows, those shows bought some groceries back then.) We even ventured out into the world to play Summer Lights and the Edmonton and Vancouver folk festivals. But sitting in the middle of that little ol' club in Green Hills always feels like home. The four of us rarely saw each other between gigs, so it was like catching up when we had a gig at the Bluebird.

As Pam and Ashley and Karen's artist careers took off, we occa-

sionally had to find a suitable substitute
to fill the empty chair. Not an easy task,
but we found great "subs" in the likes of
Beth Nielsen Chapman, Janis Ian, Marshall Chapman, and Amy Grant—not a
slouch among them!

The infamous Prom Night with Women in the Round.

Remember "Prom Night in the
Round" with the WITR dressed in for-
mals and long white gloves? Remember
the night Pam wore her Elvis-blanket
dress and could make the King's face do
all sorts of weird things? Remember
Karen's hilarious "Bad Perm Victims Benefit" and Ashley rockin' out
in the ninth month of pregnancy?

I've been to many In the Rounds, and truthfully, I've never seen
any of them with the unique chemistry that we had. Tons of fun, and
some of the greatest songs that you ever (or never) heard. Thanks to
all of the Bluebird staff and audiences throughout those ten years. It
wouldn't have worked without you all.

■ ■ ■ ■ ■

*Born and raised in Mississippi, Walker has had success in the gospel,
country, and bluegrass genres. She's toured with Connie Smith, Paul
Overstreet, and Shania Twain. Alison Krauss won a Grammy for her performance of Walker's "Looking in the Eyes of Love."*

Karen Staley

The first word that usually comes to
mind when someone mentions the
Bluebird is . . . *funny*. So when asked to
write my funniest memory of the Bluebird, I had to respond with "There are
too many to choose from!" Oddly
enough, the Bluebird was instrumental
(no pun intended) in honing my
comedic skills. It started out when I
played with the infamous Women in
the Round. There was always a bunch

*Karen Staley and Lee Satterfield raise their fists and shout
"Kid Power!" Either that or they're leading a song.*

of dead space between songs because everyone was struggling with tuning or guitar changes. So to keep the flow going I started doing little comedy bits or raffled off bizarre things I'd found during the week, like GI Joe Lip Balm. It was camouflage color and had a picture of a soldier on it. "Gee, Major, being in these desert foxholes for days on end sure is hard on a guy's lips. So you have any of that GI Joe Lip Balm in your first-aid kit?"

As I look back on over fifteen years of playing at the Bluebird, I was overcome with emotion. I realized that through all the rollercoaster ups and downs of my career, the one constant I had creatively was the Bluebird. It has always been and still is my second home.

■   ■   ■   ■   ■

After coming to Nashville from Pennsylvania, Karen Staley got work as a background vocalist for Reba McEntire. As her songwriting progressed she began to have hits with artists ranging from Tracy Byrd and Faith Hill to Patty Loveless and Michael Martin Murphy.

Pam Tillis

Women in the Round is one of my fonder musical memories. Now In the Rounds are common, but back then the only other one that had been done in Nashville was Schuyler, Knobloch, Schlitz, and Overstreet.

The cool thing for me was it happened in between record deals, so

Elvis visits the Women in the Round, giving Pam Tillis a Nutty Buddy.

I think I was feeling a little insecure, but with Women in the Round I could be in the safety of this circle, turned away from half the audience at any one time, and still be the center of attention—the perfect solution for an introverted extrovert.

I really did a lot of wood shedding there. I recut "Maybe It Was Memphis" because the response at the Bluebird to that song was so big. I had done a version for my old label that nobody dug, but I never gave up on the song because I thought if it worked that well live, it must be a hit— and it was.

Women in the Round covered so many musical and emotional bases—sultry, silly, spiritual—and the laughs could just wipe you out (Karen Staley is "not right"). My nickname was Sky King because I sang the high parts, the parts nobody else wanted.

* * * * *

Following in the footsteps of her father, Mel Tillis, Pam Tillis has proved herself a one-of-a-kind artist. An original member of Women in the Round, she's broken ground in Nashville by producing her own albums. Her hits include "One of Those Things," "Cleopatra, Queen of Denial," "Mi Vida Loca," and "It's Lonely Out There."

Ashley Cleveland

I got my start in Nashville at the Bluebird playing the Sunday Writers Nights back when a writer could sign up with Hugh Bennett in the afternoon and play the same night. I got work fairly quickly, singing on publishing demos, which I gradually parlayed into working on records as a background vocalist.

Ashley snuggled up to hubby and guitarist, Kenny Greenberg.

Highlights for me were the years of Women in the Round shows with Pam Tillis, Karen Staley, and Tricia Walker. I especially loved Prom Night when we all wore prom gowns (or, in my case, an ill-fitting bridesmaid dress), tiaras, and gloves.

I also love the memories of watching my future husband playing with the Snakes and fantasizing about him, never dreaming that we would be married with three kids. Amy and the Bluebird have been very good to me over the years.

* * * * *

A Grammy-winning artist, Ashley Cleveland puts her heart and soul into every note she sings. She was an original member of Women in the Round and has toured with such artists as John Hiatt and Amy Grant.

Marshall Chapman's Favorite Bluebird Moments

DANCING AT THE 'BIRD

Some of my happiest memories revolve around the Bluebird. I cannot remember the first time I played there, but I do remember a great recent show. It was May 23, 1999, an In the Round with Mark Collie, Lee Roy Parnell, and Brother G (Gary Nicholson). I hadn't performed in almost two years, so I was like a bird that's been released from its cage. After Matraca Berg showed up to egg us all on, spirits started running so high that nobody wanted to go home! We all ended up dancing in the back parking lot to some of Lee Roy's recently recorded Texas swing. The music was magic, pouring forth loud and clear from the speakers in Gary's fabulous car with all four doors wide open. I ended up dancing with an elderly man dressed in a tuxedo and wearing a name tag. I believe he was from Alabama.

Another time, six years or so ago, Townes Van Zandt showed up after the last note had been played of an In the Round featuring Gary Nicholson, Don Henry, Kevin Welch, and me. Townes's wife had just given birth to a baby girl at a nearby hospital, and he was out celebrating as only Townes could do. As the chairs were being set on top of the tables, a beautiful Texas waltz played on the sound system. Out of the blue, Townes, very courtly and properlike, came up and asked for my hand to dance. He carefully waltzed me around the tables. It was a moment. Townes was unique and special, and I loved him.

NEW YEARS EVE 1987

I played the 'Bird with a band—Eddie Angel, Rick Bedrosian, Dwight Scott, and Nick DiStefano. It was the first advertised non-smoking gig. Amy was initially reluctant but willing to give it a try. Of course the 'Bird was packed and nobody seemed to care. Thanks for taking a chance, Amy! You probably added ten quality years not only to my life but to the lives of countless patrons!

THE WILDEST NIGHT AT THE 'BIRD

Too many to count, but the night I played my disco Christmas song, "Who's Gonna Be My Santa Claus This Year?" at Lee Roy Parnell's Bluebird Christmas show is a definite contender. The spirit of Millie Jackson entered my body and soul as I delivered a rap beyond any I've done before or since. I've got it on tape. My favorite part is hearing Merlin Littlefield laughing in the audience.

Another memory from my wild days is when I was up onstage wearing my shortest, tightest miniskirt, playing with the Love Slaves and prancing and wobbling around in a pair of black spike heels. While introducing "Good-bye Little Rock and Roller"—you know, the part about how I wrote it while ovulating at forty thousand feet—I looked down and there was my gynecologist, Dr. Jack Cothren, sitting at the front center table! "Oh my God," I exclaimed. "Y'all won't believe this but my gynecologist is here tonight, sitting right there!" I pointed at him. Without missing a beat, I said, "You bring the stirrups, baby, and I'll bring the whips!" It's all on tape. Dr. Cothren has a copy.

THE BEST IN THE ROUND
I EVER WITNESSED

Billy Joe Shaver, Gary Nicholson, Guy Clark, and Townes Van Zandt. Say no more.

THE MOST SPECIAL
IN THE ROUND

It was 1998, Matraca Berg invited Chris (my boyfriend) and me to be her guests for a mandatory In the Round at the Bluebird as we (Matraca, Jeff, Chris, and I) were moving through the Raleigh/Durham airport on our way back to Nashville. The Round

GARY BURR

For a Yankee, Gary Burr has conquered the world of country music pretty darn effectively. This Connecticut native has seen his songs recorded by everyone from the Oak Ridge Boys to Garth Brooks, Juice Newton to Wynonna. He's been named Songwriter of the Year by *Billboard* in 1994 and by the Nashville Songwriters Association International in '94 and '95. And he's gotten to play guitar for a Beatle.

Gary picked up the guitar while in a cast, the result of a broken leg from playing soccer in high school. After experiencing Woodstock, he and a friend decided they could do the same thing they were witnessing onstage. He began to send demos of his songs to record companies ... and to get rejected. Finally, however, he got a recording contract and joined Pure Prairie League in 1980 as guitarist and lead singer. Gary began to send his songs to Nashville and hit the bull's-eye with his very first attempt when Juice Newton recorded his tune "Love's Been a Little Bit Hard on Me," taking it to number seven on the pop charts. That was soon followed by a number-one smash, "Make My Life with You," recorded by the Oaks. Gary began making trips to Nashville and was a frequent special guest on our Sunday writers' showcase.

Gary moved to Nashville in 1989, and the hits kept coming. His Bluebird appearances increased as well. The Burr, Bob DiPiero, Jim Photoglo, and Russell Smith In the Rounds have rivaled the original In the Round and Women in the Round in popularity and longevity. He's also

(continued)

would feature her, Beth Neilsen Chapman, Gary Burr, and a "secret guest." I tried to get her to tell me who the secret guest was, but Matraca can keep a secret. After a while, I finally gave up. By then we were riding one of those "people mover" escalator things when out of the blue I started singing: "I feel the earth move under my feet/I feel the sky tumbling down." Matraca's eyes got real big, but she never said a word. Yes, it turned out Carole King was the secret guest. On the night of the show, I sat right across from Carole and sang along on "Smackwater Jack." On "Will You Still Love Me Tomorrow," I unashamedly wept. Matraca now thinks I'm psychic.

OTHER MOMENTS

Dion DiMucci's ("Runaround Sue," "Teenager in Love") manager, Zack Glickman, heard me sing my and Brother G's "The 90's Is the 60's Turned Upside Down," one of the first times I ever played it live. It was at the Bluebird in 1990. After the set he asked me to send him a cassette of the song. I did, then thought nothing more of it. Until I came home one day and heard Dion unmistakably talking on my code-a-phone, telling me how much he loved the song. His Brooklyn accent killed me: "Maah-shul, I love dat song, Maah-shul! I could sing dat song with one lip tied behind my back, Maah-shul." He cut it and it ended up on his *Hearts on Fire* album.

The Love Slaves and I played the Bluebird on a snowy January night in 1991. It was my birthday. Because of the heavy snow, there was hardly anyone in the audi-

GARY BURR

put together a band of crack session musicians and often makes a monthly appearance onstage rather than In the Round.

With his successes multiplying in the country field, Gary has branched out in recent years and begun writing with pop artists like Carole King and Michael Bolton and members of Aerosmith. He also produced *The Best of Country Sing Disney*, a Nashville tribute to the music of Disney films.

Gary will tell you that his career highlight so far has been the chance to work with Ringo Starr as a guitarist in his band. They taped a VH1 *Storytellers* show and played several more dates in support of Ringo's most recent album.

Due to popular demand, Gary finally released an album of his own in 1997. *Stop Me If You've Heard This One . . .* was recorded live in front of a studio audience at Sunset Studios in Nashville and features eighteen Burr compositions. We were thrilled to watch Gary's career explode in the nineties and equally thrilled that he's shared so much of his time and talent with the Bluebird.

Here's a partial list of Gary's hits:

"Sure Love"
"I Try to Think About Elvis"
"In a Week or Two"
"I Wear Your Love"
"Out of My Bones"
"I Already Do"
" 'Til You Love Me"
"One Night a Day"
"That's My Job"
"What's in It for Me"
"On the Side of Angels"

ence, except for Duane Eddy, who'd parked himself right in front of Eddie Angel's amp. We rocked!

May 6, 1993: The night LeRoy Neiman was in the audience with his trademark handlebar moustache and his sketch pad. I was playing In the Round with Jamie O'Hara, Brother G, and Don Henry. Jon Ims and Gary Burr sat in, and LeRoy did a wonderful series of sketches of all of us. Signed photostat copies now hang in Brother G's studio, in my office, and at the 'Bird.

∎　∎　∎　∎

Marshall Chapman is equal parts Southern charm and Southern attitude. Her major-label releases in the seventies laid the groundwork for many of the strong, independent female voices in rock today. Sawyer Brown put a country spin on her song "Betty's Bein' Bad" and made it a hit.

ROUNDS "R" US

Once the "one-round only" barrier had been broken, it seemed like everyone wanted to experience this new way to play the Bluebird. As rounds became in demand we began to have as many as four a week, with several rivaling Schuyler, Knobloch, Bickhardt, and Schlitz and Women in the Round in their popularity. The Gary Burr, Bob DiPiero, Jim Photoglo, and Russell Smith group is one of the best, in terms of both hits and hilarity. Carl Jackson, Larry Cordle, Jim Rushing, and Waylon Patton put a bluegrass spin on the rounds they played. The warmth and intimacy of playing the Bluebird in

Suzy Bogguss, Beth Nielsen Chapman, Matraca Berg, and Gretchen Peters showing the effects of a particularly memorable In the Round.

the round is so inviting, even the Floating Men, one of Nashville's best-loved alternative bands, insisted on doing a show in that format.

Of course that intimacy can turn to intimidation for seasoned performers used to big stages and a wide space between them and the audience. We've seen more than a handful of "big names" (we won't name any) called upon to do a song or two and become totally nervous and flustered. In the Round has become a proving ground for songwriters. It's just them and a guitar. The songs have to stand on their own. The writers know it, and it's probably one of the reasons they love In the Round so much. Whether one is performing or listening, In the Round is Songwriting 101 and pure inspiration.

Tony Arata

So that I could pursue songwriting, my wife, Jaymi, and I packed up our belongings and moved here from Savannah, Georgia, on Halloween of 1986. We spent the next day unloading a huge rental truck

Tony Arata trades tunes with the man who almost made him go home, Don Schlitz.

and decided that we would call it a day, get cleaned up, and go down to the Bluebird to see what the local competition was like. It was packed, but Jaymi and I found a place along the back wall. We saw four gentlemen (I use the term loosely) sitting in the middle of the room playing and singing. They were Thom Schuyler, Don Schlitz, Fred Knobloch, and Craig Bickhardt. Every song that each of them did was either currently on the radio or had already proven itself a major, major hit in the recent months. I began to get a sick feeling in my stomach, and I asked Jaymi if we could go. She asked, "Do you want to go home?"

I said, "Yes, I want to go home—*to Savannah.*"

■   ■   ■   ■   ■

Garth Brooks gave Tony Arata his first big hit with his cover of "The Dance." Subsequent hits came with Patty Loveless recording "Here I Am" and "A Handful of Dust." Lee Roy Parnell hit the charts with Tony's "Holding My Own," and Clay Walker made it big with "Dreaming with My Eyes Wide Open."

Beth Nielsen Chapman

I'll never forget my first performance at the Bluebird. I was fresh off the turnip truck and waltzed in, having been allotted a small slot to play a song between the two sets of Schuyler, Knobloch, Schlitz, and Overstreet. I had not a clue about the legendary status of these writers, nor did I appreciate the extremely unusual opportunity I had been given, being new in town, to appear on the same stage with these guys. It was only as a favor to my new publisher, Meredith Stuart, that they agreed to let me perform. In addition to my obliviousness, I came in late and unfortunately missed the first set, which should have clued me in that I was a little in over my head. I got there just in time to jump up onstage and do my thing. I was a bit surprised after singing the first song, which, incidentally, should have been my only song, to sense a somewhat cool response from the audience. I'd never had that happen back home! So I figured I'd better do another song so I could at least grab them and make a good impression. Well, the second song was even more painful. It was clear to me that I was being tolerated by an audience that came to see the other guys. Incredibly, I did a third song—sort of as a last-ditch effort. And then I slunk off stage in a state of disappointment and confusion.

Still somewhat clueless in spite of my flop performance, I wandered over to Thom Schuyler just before they went back on for their second set and managed to further put my foot in my mouth. After a short "Hello, how are you?" I said, "So, would you like to cowrite a song sometime?" He gracefully smiled and somehow made it to the stage without putting a date on the books. The real clincher came when I settled down with my Corona and heard their set. Every song was so strong; several of them had already been hits. All of a sudden, to my embarrassment, I realized I'd been on another planet. It wasn't until almost a year later that I had the opportunity to write "Strong Enough to Bend" with Don Schlitz, and one night, at one of the earliest In the Round nights, he invited me to come into the circle and do that song. And I was invited to stay and sing a second one. I had come to many realizations in that year and was just starting to really feel comfortable in this town swimming with songwriters. Mostly I had developed an appreciation for all the talented people here and all that I could learn from them. I also found that songwriters are a forgiving bunch and while there is competition, there's also a great support system for growth and improvement.

■   ■   ■   ■   ■

Beth Nielsen Chapman cut her teeth playing the lounges and clubs of Mobile, Alabama. After moving to Nashville she found success as a writer of hits like "Strong Enough to Bend," "Nothing I Can Do About It Now," and "Down on My Knees." As a recording artist she's released four albums on the Reprise label and had an Adult/Contemporary chart hit with "In the Time It Takes." Her moving tribute to her late husband, Ernest, "Sand and Water," was chosen by Elton John to honor Princess Diana in his concerts. Her later hits include "This Kiss" and "Happy Girl."

Gary Burr

I would like to say that my first time playing the Bluebird is my most vivid memory because the 'Bird has meant so much to me. Or I could tell you about all the wonderful writers I've heard and played with over the years. But no.

It's Bob DiPiero wearing Tweety Bird Pajamas, Jimmy Photoglo

Chely Wright joins the boys in their jammies at Gary Burr's Pajama Party.

in black garters and a *Raging Bull* T-shirt. Russell Smith in a smoking jacket looking like David Niven. Mama Price in full facial mask and curlers. Anna W. in cute jammies with little feet on them . . . and me in a purple negligee. I will do anything for a laugh, but I had no idea that once the evening began I would be pulling up the shoulder straps all night and watching Russell's eyebrows go up every time I crossed my legs. Pizzas ordered for the club by cell phone at midnight, an alarm clock set to tell us when to break—and when it went off in the middle of my ballad "Can't Be Really Gone," we stopped and took a break.

That's my memory. I love the Bluebird and the friends in my life that it helped me make. Your closing will leave a hole in my . . . oh, you're not closing? What the hell did I write this for?

* * * * *

Gary Burr was undoubtedly the most successful songwriter in country music in the nineties. His string of hits is amazing. Warming up in the eighties with Juice Newton's version of "Love's Been a Little Bit Hard on Me," Gary went on to pen the hits "Sure Love," "What Mattered Most," "In a Week or Two," "One Night a Day," "On the Side of Angels," "Can't Be Really Gone," "Out of My Bones," and so many more. The first Gary Burr Birthday Pajama Party took place in February of '93. It's become an annual tradition.

Jim Photoglo

The Bluebird Cafe has been the site of many firsts for me since I moved to Nashville in 1985. Whether it was a songwriter showcase, a new band, or a new stage outfit, it felt like the most comfortable place to try things out. The fabulous Del Beatles and Run C&W premiered there. I had never performed in pajamas until we began THE Annual Birthday Pajama Party. Then there was Halloween night in 1998, when I came dressed as Gary Burr.

The club attracts a varied clientele. I met former presidential advisor George Stephanopoulos and budding songwriter/convicted murderer Paul Reid there. He said, "I got this killer idea . . ."

* * * * *

Remember "We Were Meant to Be Lovers"? That was the pop hit that launched Jim Photoglo's career. Of course that was back in L.A., where he was known simply as Photoglo. After coming to Nashville he reclaimed his first name and went to work writing great songs like "Hillbilly Hollywood," "Fishing in the Dark," and "Silence Is King Around Here." He recently released a new album entitled Fly Straight Home.

Bob DiPiero

One night at the Bluebird there was an extra good Women in the Round. One of the performers was Amy Grant. I sat with my back against the window. Amy saw me and invited me up to play a song. So

This might be the biggest round we've ever had, pound for pound. Randy Bachman (holding the guitar) of BTO and the Guess Who is joined by former NRBQ guiatrist Al Anderson and songwriters Craig Wiseman and Bob DiPiero.

there I sat with Ashley Cleveland, Beth Neilsen Chapman, Karen Staley, and Amy Grant. Amy offered me her chair and her guitar to play. The place was packed, no room to breathe, let alone find an extra chair. So Amy proceeded to sit on the floor, at my feet, looking up at me. You've got to remember, I was married to Pam Tillis at the time. I think I had a stroke. I can't remember what I sang, if I sucked or if anyone applauded. All that curly brown hair and these angel eyes had pretty much paralyzed me. Actually, I'm just now starting to remember most of this. I know what it was! I was having a chick-singer attack. I was surrounded, and I couldn't get out. Get out? Hell. I was trying to figure out a way to get 'em all in One Big Area.

The future of fashion in country music? Vince Melamed, Bob DiPiero, Gary Burr, and Jim Photoglo are ready.

One of my favorite Bluebird In the Round foursomes included Gary Burr, Jim Photoglo, and the G. Gordon Liddy of Hillbilly Music, Russell Smith. Gary had started a yearly tradition of having a pajama party at the Bluebird on or near his birthday. This was in front of a paying audience. The first year we all wore some form of nighttime attire, and we invited the audience to join in. I'll never forget the sight of brand-new artist Faith Hill, sitting there watching us in flannel PJ's and little fluffy bunny slippers. Who needs Victoria's Secret when you've got Faith Hill in fluffy bunny slippers smiling at you and singing along?

Anyway, the next year was a serious escalation in PJ's for the performers. Photoglo showed up in a red flannel union suit with a trap door in the back and a long matching nightcap. Horror

Russell Smith, Jim Photoglo, and Gary Burr do their best to replicate the missing Bob DiPiero.

of horrors, Russell also showed up in a red union suit—with the trap door slightly open. His PJ's were set off by some muddy cowboy boots and what looked like a potato stuck in his shorts.

Not to be outdone, Gary Burr was absolutely lovely, if not fetching, wearing a pale blue chiffon peekaboo nightie with a scoop neckline. The sight of him sitting at the Bluebird in his chiffon nightie singing "Can't Be Really Gone" drove me into years of therapy.

Yours truly, Bobby D., rose to the occasion. I had a pair of pajamas specially made for me by my soon-to-be-former wife's (Pam) sister Carrie. XXL of course. They were bright Kaopectate pink with yellow Tweety Birds all over the material. Little blue plastic pacifiers acted as buttons for these atomic PJ's.

So I sat there in my pink Tweety Bird PJ's drinking Jägermeister and singing "Church on Cumberland Road" at the Bluebird—and they say we don't take our profession seriously. Ha! *(See Bob's bio on page 43.)*

Bill Lloyd

Just a few years ago I was playing an In the Round with Rodney Crowell, Beth Nielsen Chapman, and Kimmie Rhodes. Because they were all good friends with Waylon Jennings, Waylon attended the show that evening. Lucky for all of us that night, he didn't mind coming up and joining in for a couple of rounds. After getting settled in and doing his first song, he looked a little restless and jokingly asked the crowd, "What are y'all lookin' at?" Beth looked over at him and said, "Well, you *are* Waylon Jennings." It hit me again how

Yes, he is Waylon Jennings.

safe and comfortable it feels when you're playing on big stages with a rehearsed band backing you up, traveling from city to city and show to show. Something about playing an acoustic guitar and singing straight off the cuff in the middle of a room surrounded by strangers can rattle your nerves more than playing to thousands. It's often the truth of those performances that makes it likely that you'll hear something life-changing when you attend these songwriter shows. The lack of show biz is more than just refreshing—it's essential.

． ． ． ． ． ．

Bill Lloyd was dragging country music into the twenty-first century long before the world heard the names Garth and Shania. As one half of Foster & Lloyd, he was putting rock and pop influences into his songs while still keeping just the right amount of twang. His hits include "Crazy Over You," "Sure Thing," and "I Keep Coming Back to You."

Jim Messina, of Loggins and Messina fame, has done a few very special rounds at the Bluebird. Here he is with a very happy Ashley Cleveland.

David Crosby of CSN and Buffalo Springfield dropped by to do a few songs In the Round ... and maybe to talk about surrogate fatherhood.

Don Henry

From the first time to the last, it's always a memorable experience playing the Bluebird Cafe. You'll see the best writers in the world on any given night. Us local cronies can get a bit perturbed at the occasional *shhh!* that the Bluebird is infamous for. But where else in the world can you go play and listen to the newest by the greatest? A little silence is in order, don't you think? That said, my favorite nights are the ones that *rock!* (So what the hell do I know about *shhh!*)

I remember a night with Bill Lloyd, Pat Buchanan, and Rusty Young—enough of a reason to be starstruck already—then Jim Messina shows up and does "Kind Woman" from his Buffalo Springfield days (my favorite American band). Of course Rusty played steel on that record as a young man. I remember Bill's and Pat's ear-to-ear grins as they finally got to play their "Springfield licks" in the context of the real thing! The only thing missing for me were the vinyl pops that my ears had grown so accustomed to through the years.

Bill Lloyd (Nashville's Father of Power Pop) brings good luck to Bluebird In the Rounds. On a night not long after this episode, David Crosby and Bernie Leadon slipped in while I was playing with Bill, Waylon Patton, and Kostas. We invited them up, and Bernie accompanied David on a couple of new tunes as well as a couple of classics. David borrowed Bill's guitar until he broke a string while he was tuning for "Guinevere," so he had to use my guitar for his finale. He sang like a bird, and my Guild never sounded better.

From the Braddocks to the Prines, from the Delberts to the Hiatts, you just never know who'll show up next. Here's to forever and the Bluebird Cafe.

■ ■ ■ ■ ■

Bluebird audiences will tell you there's no one else quite like Don Henry. A California native, he's able to touch hearts and tickle funny bones in the same song. He also manages to write memorable hits like "Where've You Been," "A Whole Lotta Holes," "BFD," "Has Anybody Seen Amy?" and "Back on the Farm Again."

Gary Harrison

I guess all of us have experienced magic moments at the Bluebird. For me, I recall a particular night a couple of years ago. I was playing an In the Round with Don Henry, Keith Stegall, and Harley Allen. Everything was working that night. The crowd was with us, everyone sounded good, a general good feeling hung in the air.

Don capped the evening off by playing "Where've You Been." It was truly moving. I sat there, not as a pro song-

Here's Don Henry surrounded by Bill Lloyd and Dave Olney.

writer and grizzled Music Row rat but as someone in love with songs and in awe of Don's gifts. The audience gave him a standing ovation, and Don stood up, obviously moved himself, to acknowledge the audience.

It was then that I noticed (as I'm sure everyone but Don did) that his pants were unzipped and his fly was wide open. Gotta love Don Henry!

■　■　■　■　■

Gary Harrison has written two big hits for Trisha Yearwood: "Wrong Side of Memphis" and "Everybody Knows." He's also penned hit songs for Doug Stone, Mark Chesnutt, and Martina McBride.

Hugh Prestwood

I've had *many* great times at the Bluebird. I guess the one that stands out the most is the night I performed with Julie Gold, Mike Reid,

Hugh Prestwood giving a lesson in hit songwriting.

and Gary Burr, during Tin Pan South a few years ago. About ten minutes before we were to start, Bonnie Raitt came in. The energy in the room immediately went through the roof, and I began to rethink what songs I was going to play, on the assumption that anyone as important as Bonnie would not stay for the whole show. But much to my amazement and delight, she stayed the whole night, played a few songs, and, to top it off, came up to me afterward and was very generous in her praise of my songwriting. If I had that conversation on videotape, I'd play it about once a week. It was a magical night. I might add that about 90 percent of the magical nights I have ever had performing have been at the Bluebird.

■　■　■　■　■

Hugh Prestwood is living proof that some of Nashville's best writers don't live in Nashville. Prestwood resides just outside of New York City, but he knows what Nashville wants and continues to provide it with songs like "Ghost in This House," "The Song Remembers When," "Hard Rock Bottom of Your Heart," and "That's That."

■　■　■　■　■

We've always known that our audiences loved the In the Round experience, but we didn't know just how far they would go to prove it until one couple showed us.

Scott Lee

I didn't really mean to do it, but in September 1994 while sitting at dinner my spirit overwhelmed my mind and I asked Linda to marry me. Unaware of the marriage tax, we set a December 17 date.

It turns out that churches are pretty busy that time of year and all of the other places we could think of were booked too. So she suggested the Bluebird. I misunderstood and said that would be a great place for a reception. She hung in there until I got the idea that the Bluebird would be a perfect spot for our wedding ceremony.

Amy Kurland was an absolute joy of a hostess, and the food is still being talked about by our family and friends. We were married In the Round at the world-famous Bluebird Cafe. What a celebration we had!

Amy Grant

The Bluebird is a great listening room. Its "no talking" reputation is legendary. And an evening of music there is a pleasure for songwriters and song lovers alike.

One night I invited my three sisters and a couple of friends to see Ashley Cleveland, Karen Staley, Pam Tillis, and Tricia Walker do a Women in the Round.

The no-talking issue was discussed beforehand, since we were a table full of women and talking is what we do. Anyway, jokes were flying, estrogen levels were soaring, and I took the opportunity to lean over the candlelit table to whisper something to my sister.

Who knows what's in hair products these days, but that candle flame leaped up about six inches and caught my hair on fire. Without a word, almost without a sound, two glasses of liquid were thrown at my little fireball—one water, one wine—and after a lot of quick swatting, the flames were out.

Not a sound came from our table to interrupt the song in

midstream, just a burnt, pungent smell that made our appetizers less appealing. A smell that brought a few comments from the songwriters during the next round of banter. Starting with "What is that?!"

"SHHH . . . shhh . . . shhh" . . . Long live the listening room.

■　■　■　■　■

Amy Grant crossed over from gospel music to become a pop sensation in the 1990s. Hits like "Baby Baby" and "House of Love" have made her a mainstay on radio and VH1. Her In the Round audiences are struck by her humor and humility.

CHAPTER 4

THE BLUEBIRD TAKES FLIGHT

BLUEBIRD SHOWS ON THE ROAD

With a name like Bluebird, it's only right that we should eventually leave our comfortable little nest here in Nashville and take the In the Round format to festivals, clubs, private business functions, and even the occasional airport.

Pam Tillis

The worst gig was the airport here in Nashville. It was supposed to be some

The Canal Street Tavern in Dayton, Ohio, is a familiar venue to a lot of the touring artists who come to the Bluebird. The Women in the Round included it in one of their minitours.

"Takin' it to the street." Before the gig in Dayton, Pam, Karen, and Tricia run wild.

When Amy takes a show to the Bottom Line she also takes some friends along, too. Here Julia Harrison and Katie McCoy visit the famous New York venue.

At the Bottom Line, Hal Ketchum signs an autograph for a fan.

kind of "support the arts in the airport" deal, but I was so embarrassed that I kept hiding behind this big potted fern in the concourse. Needless to say, I was happy to get back to the Bluebird when that debacle was all over. *(See Pam's bio on page 52.)*

Okay, so maybe the airport gig wasn't the best idea. We just had to support the arts. We've had much better luck taking our Bluebird shows to other venues.

Schuyler, Knobloch, and Schlitz were our first Bluebird ambassadors, taking the In the Round format to the Old Town School of Folk Music in Chicago. The Women in the Round soon followed suit, offering up their luscious harmonies at the Vancouver Folk Festival in Canada, the Canal Street Tavern in Dayton, Ohio, and several other locations.

When Amy first approached Allan Pepper at the Bottom Line about trading shows, Pepper didn't think the New York audiences would be overly interested in Nashville songwriters. But once the idea of creating shows built around Grammy nominees was hit upon, a tradition was born. Since the start of the nineties, Amy's Bluebird Grammy Nights at the Bottom Line have featured a veritable who's who of Nashville's elite. Amy Grant, Foster & Lloyd, Kim Richey, Trisha Yearwood, Gillian Welch, Kathy Mattea, Hugh Prestwood, and Julie Gold have all delighted audiences in the West Village landmark. When the Grammys moved to Los Angeles in '99, Amy took her show to the Bluebird/Bottom Line equivalent in L.A., the Troubadour.

In 1996 Disney World opened the Disney Institute, which celebrates creativity by showcasing the creative arts. The Bluebird was on hand with Amy Grant, Wayne Kirkpatrick, Bob DiPiero, Gary Burr, Hugh Prestwood, and Julie Gold. We took shows there through June 2000.

The marquee tells the tale outside the cinema at the Disney Institute.

Allen Shamblin

On February 19, 2000, Angela Kaset, Steve Seskin, and I performed at the Disney Institute in Orlando as part of the Bluebird Songwriter Series.

After the show, a Magic Kingdom "host" (who has requested to remain nameless) introduced himself to my wife, Lori, in the gift shop. This kind man had spotted Lori and our children (Ashli, Caleb, and Lindsey) in the balcony when I mentioned from the stage that this was the kids' first time seeing me perform in front of an audience.

He said that he wanted to do something special for the kids, but he asked us to keep it a secret until he could work out the logistics. The next morning we got a phone call confirming that our family would be the grand marshals of the Magic Kingdom Parade.

The Shamblin family sprouts Tigger ears as the grand marshalls of Disney World's Magic Kingdom Parade.

I was half hoping that Robin, our hostess for the day, was kidding when she handed me a pair of Tigger ears and said I had to wear them if I wanted to ride in the parade. But when I looked over and into the faces of three of the happiest children in the world, I put those Tigger ears on and wore 'em with pride. It was truly a magical moment and a day our family will always remember. *(See Allen's bio on page 30.)*

The year 1999 saw the Bluebird take In the Round to the Tabernacle in Atlanta. Formerly the site of the House of Blues during the '96 Summer

Olympics, the Tabernacle is a three-thousand-seat club located in downtown Atlanta, across from Centennial Park. Our shows took place in the Cellar, the 120-seat restaurant in the lower level. It was this series of shows that led the Turner South Network to develop the idea for *Live from the Bluebird Cafe*. Producer Jim May has been here for every one of the tapings. We'll let Jim and his partner, Catherine, tell the story.

Jim May and Catherine Fleming

Amy Kurland called in the spring of 1999 and said TBS was starting a new cable channel and wanted to do a music show from her club. She wanted the show to reflect the intimacy and camaraderie that has been the trademark of the Bluebird Cafe.

Working with Amy, we were able to find a way to set up a four-camera shoot in the already cramped quarters of the Bluebird Cafe without intruding on the performers, without distracting the audience, and without major interference with the workings of the restau-

Hanging out in the back hallway (where they really shouldn't be) are Clint Black, actor David Keith, and Joe Ely.

rant. We signed on to do twenty-two shows for Turner South, a division of Time Warner, now AOL Time Warner.

In January 2001 we completed shooting our second season of *Live from the Bluebird Cafe*. There are now forty-five hourlong shows presenting 112 songwriters performing 443 songs. Another 200 cowriters are represented.

Our greatest satisfaction has come from knowing that we are archiving some great Nashville treasures and that

we are giving an opportunity for others to see and experience the great wealth of talent we have here. Not only do we have recordings of the songs that have been used in the show, but we have recordings of another six hundred songs that may end up on a compilation tape or in shows yet to edited. We have songs that were major hits and songs of the year, and we have new songs that have yet to be recorded. We have some songs that are so fresh a verse is forgotten or is conjured on the spot.

There are songs that make you want to cry, like Gene Nelson's "For the Scars" or "In My Secret Life" and Jon Vezner's version of

"Where've You Been," and songs that make you laugh—Marshall Chapman's "Just to Torture Myself" and Cheryl Wheeler's "Potato."

Then there are the perfect songs, the perfect moments: Shawn Mullins and Larry Jon Wilson singing "Loose Change" or "Friday Night Fights at Al's Place"; Julie Miller crooning "Broken Things"; Bobby Braddock pounding out the acerbic "Same Old Song" and then silencing the room with "He Stopped Loving Her Today"; Dave Olney singing "Deeper Well," accompanied by Kieran Kane and Kevin Welch; Don Schlitz's performance of "On the Other Hand," which is turned into a free-for-all by Fred Knobloch's outrageous guitar licks and Thom Schuyler's added "talking verses."

There are the incredible guitars: Buddy Miller, one of the best pickers in Nashville, doing "Somewhere Trouble Don't Go"; guitar Buddha Al Anderson with Jeffrey Steele and Kent Blazy burning it up on "Pour Me" or "Something in the Water"; keith urban's foot frantically beating against the floor as he rocks to "Shelby County Jail"; Marcus Hummon's intro to "Shining Son"; Fred Knobloch's "Feels Like Mississippi"; Lee Roy Parnell with Joe Ely on "Milk Cow Blues"; Chuck Jones on "S-a-t-u-r-d-a-y Night"; and Gary Nicholson's intro to "Memphis Women and Chicken."

And then the stories: Delbert McClinton telling us about living in a place called Methadrine Manor while writing "Two More Bottles of Wine"; Allen Shamblin charming the room with stories from his children: "Daddy, did you ever used to have a job?" and then letting us in on the story behind the creation of "I Can't Make You Love Me"; Bob DiPiero's "Blue Clear Sky" story; a tipsy Matraca Berg pitching Don Henry's "Motel" to an imaginary George Strait; Paul Williams's candor about his recovery from alcohol abuse and how he made it through a writing session with Barbra Streisand to emerge with "Evergreen," or about how his mother inspired the first line of "Rainy Days and Mondays"; Joe Ely recounting his days as a roofer, and how he once took a roof off the wrong house; Rodney Crowell

Mickey Newbury tunes up as Delbert McClinton looks on.

speaking delicately about his father in the intro of "Rock of My Soul"; Kim Ritchie musing on the first time she heard one of her songs at the Home Depot and how she came to meet Bill Lloyd back in college;

73

Sharon Vaughn on how she pitched "My Heroes Have Always Been Cowboys" to Waylon Jennings and how he recorded it that night. There are so many great stories.

And then there are the shows that just have it all—the songs, the stories, the banter, the laughs, and the tears. There is the sheer beauty

of exceptional shows like Buddy and Julie Miller with Jim Lauderdale, or Shawn Mullins with his Augustan mentor, Larry Jon Wilson, or Matraca Berg and Marshall Chapman with Don Henry, or keith urban, Leslie Satcher, and Harley Allen, or Guy Clark and Verlon Thompson with Hal Ketchum. There's the Emmy-nominated show featuring Delbert McClinton, Rodney Crowell, and Gary Nicholson where Gary starts a round of songs dedicated

Hal Ketchum seems to get better (and better-looking) all the time.

to their wives. Gary does "Better Word for Love," Rodney does "Tied to You"—both beautiful ballads—and Delbert follows with "If You Can't Lie No Better Than That (You Might As Well Tell the Truth)."

Producing the show has been an absolute joy. A family has been created on the nights we shoot. We have a crew that has been constant and looks forward to each night of taping. We have great camera operators and technicians. We are grateful for Suzanne Carter's limited lighting, Carol Frazier's light touch on makeup, and Vaughn Skow's multitrack recording and subsequent mix of the shows. Amy's staff at the Bluebird, from John Mark and the lovely Didi at the door to Keith and John in the kitchen, from Alison and the Jennifers to the rock-steady Tony at the bar and Phil at the house sound booth—all have embraced us and made us feel very welcome in their "living room." They are all regular stars of the show, and their grace and warmth have been very appreciated.

The writers and performers who have shared their songs with us also enjoy taping the show. They may come to sound check a little apprehensive, and they may be a bit nervous when we start the evening, but when the night is done, there seems to be a unanimous feeling that it was fun and that during the course of the evening they came close to forgetting that they were doing a television show. This is when we know we've done it right.

Our third season began taping in July 2001.

■ ■ ■ ■ ■

Jim May has over twenty years' experience producing and directing award-winning commercials, videos, and television programs. He is a co-founder of RuckusFilm. His video credits include: Alan Jackson, Patty Loveless, Aerosmith, Clint Black, and Kathy Mattea.

Catherine Fleming is a Nashville native and a cofounder of RuckusFilm. She is also a producer, director, production manager, editor, videographer, casting director, and photographer. Her video credits include: Limp Bizkit, Deana Carter, Swan Dive, Shawn Mullins, and the Newsboys.

In the last few years we've also taken our "Bluebird on the Road" to the Folk Alliance Conference in Memphis and Albuquerque. We've also found ourselves in demand for many corporate affairs. Federal judges, nuclear engineers, and pharmaceutical representatives have all opted for the Bluebird In the Round experience to make their gatherings memorable and enjoyable. One such night at the 'Bird led to what is, so far, our farthest-reaching flight.

Marc-Alan Barnette

In a club like the 'Bird that is filled with so many stories, it's hard to pick just one. The Bluebird not only gave me my start in Nashville but also introduced me to what being a singer-songwriter is all about. So here is my favorite.

After playing seven years at the 'Bird in every conceivable fashion and configuration, I moved up to being on its private-party list. This is where some of the better-known songwriters do private parties to introduce the outside, corporate world to what the Bluebird is really about: original music in its purest form. I was pretty honored to be chosen, however, the time, eight o'clock on a Sunday morning, was a bit of a stretch for an entertainer.

Kongar Al-ondar from the Mongolian region of Russia. He amazed a Bluebird audience with his display of what is known as Tuvan throat singing in which multiple notes are produced at the same time.

The crowd that morning was an interesting lot. They were fifty travel agents from around the world. France, England, Spain, the

Netherlands, Sweden, and Denmark were all represented. Their bus pulled up, and they ambled off and began drinking around nine. This of course was nine at night for them, so it was quite normal.

I got things up and going and around the second song realized that some of them didn't even speak English. But they were for the most part polite, attentive, and actually a lot of fun. Except for one guy. He sat in the corner, kind of glum, looking like a foggy British afternoon and like he wanted to be somewhere else. So I kind of ignored him.

At the break he came over to me, and as I was expecting the "What is your real job?" question, he asked in a thick, French-sounding accent, " 'Ave you ever thought ovvvv going to Beljuum-mmn?"

"Yeah, right," I thought. It's an everyday occurrence to finish that big afternoon set at Tootsie's, hop into your limo, and head to Brussels! So I kind of played it down and sent him to the manager.

Three weeks later would find me, the three other performers, and our chaperone sitting on a plane bound for Europe. We spent three incredible days in Brussels, met the most wonderful people, and got to share our songs with a truly international audience. So I got to be a goodwill ambassador for the Bluebird, songwriting, and music in General. Where else but the Bluebird does that happen?

It's the epitome of what I got into music for in the first place. Sharing yourselves with as many people as you can. It is an honor. It is the Bluebird.

■　■　■　■　■

Marc-Alan Barnette has a voice that will blow you away. His brand of "in-your-face rockin' country" is reminiscent of the best of Ronnie Milsap and Lee Roy Parnell. He tours extensively and has released several independent albums.

Most recently we've been doing a series of Bluebird Cafe In the Round shows at a venue in Roswell, Georgia, known as the Swallow in the Hollow. Proprietor Bill Greenwood approached Amy about bringing our writers to his club, and she, of course, agreed. Everyone from Fred Knobloch, Tony Arata, and Thom Schuyler to Bernie Nelson, Russell Smith, and Vince Melamed have done this 150-seat venue located about twenty miles outside of Atlanta. The response has been fabulous.

CHAPTER 5

FOR THE BENEFIT OF...

KIDS BELONG IN NIGHTCLUBS

The Milk and Cookies Concert Series

After being in business for six years or so, we realized there was an important demographic whose entertainment dollar was not making it into our cash register: preschoolers. Okay so they don't really have an entertainment dollar to spend, but we found a way to get them into the Bluebird. More specifically, Henry Cory found a way, and the way is our Milk and Cookies Concert Series.

Henry is a former clown and writer

As the sugar kicks in, the kids take control of the club. Or at least one pushover of a soundman.

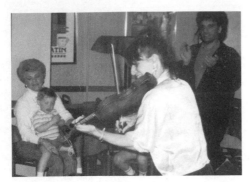

*Henry Cory stands in the background as a guest performer
fiddles her way into the kids' hearts.*

Someone said "cookies" and the stampede began.

This is what it's all about. Look at those smiles.

of children's songs and books. It was
his idea to do a monthly children's
show. In the beginning, they were held
on Saturdays and included a small
cover charge to cover the cost of milk
and a peanut-butter-and-jelly sandwich. Amy, however, envisioned a show
that brought together kids from both
sides of Nashville's tracks. The show
was moved to Thursdays, and the mix
of children became more diverse. Kids
from underpriviledged households sat
side by side with kids from upper-
income Belle Meade neighborhoods
and learned that they had a lot more
in common than they might have
thought.

Over the years the Milk and Cookies
Series has brought in a broad range of
teachers and talent to entertain and edu-
cate Nashville's next generation. We've
had dentists, firemen (a fire truck too),
veterinarians, and even Hawaiian hula
dancers. Along the way, a few of our
regular Bluebird performers found out
it takes a completely different approach
to hold the attention of a roomful of
preschoolers. Some only tried it once.
Still, it's not who's onstage that matters.
It's the kids, eyes lit up, cookie crumbs
on their lips, and a brand-new song still
spinning in their heads, that make the
Milk and Cookies show a joy to do each
month.

LET'S SEE SOME ID, GRAMPS

The For Seniors Only Concerts

Get a bar full of senior citizens, add sugar and caffeine, and you're just asking for trouble . . . but we did it anyway. Our For Seniors Only concerts were the brainchild of Katy McCoy, a former waitress and bartender at the Bluebird. An elderly friend of Katy's was losing his sight and staying in an assisted-living facility. During one of her usual visits he told Katy one of the things he missed most was going out to hear live music. Thus was born the For Seniors Only concert series, a way for seniors to get out and enjoy live music without having to deal with late nights, loud bands, and smoky bars. They've been a huge success, a treat for the seniors and the writers who come in to perform for them.

"We thought this was a Chippendale's show."

The sharp-dressed man in cheap sunglasses, ZZ Top's Billy Gibbons, trading photos with former waitress Iny Patterson and bartender Katy McCoy.

Gene Pistilli

To me, the Bluebird Cafe is the Grand Ole Opry for songwriters. On its stage I've seen some of the great writers of all time sing some of the great songs of all time. I've also had the privilege of performing there myself. I particularly enjoy doing Amy's senior citizen shows with my good friends Teddy Irwin and Fats Kaplan. We get to play real traditional country-and-western swing for an audience who sings along with "You Are My Sunshine" and "Mexicali Rose"! Thanks, Amy, for the lovely memories you've given me, and here's to a whole lot more.

■ ■ ■ ■ ■

Gene Pistilli was an original member of Manhattan Transfer. His love for jazz and swing is evident in his tunes "Too Good to Be True" and "Sure Feels Real Good."

Henry Gross

I've had many wonderful nights of music at the Bluebird—as a listener, a band member, a solo performer, and a member of a writer In the Round group with some of my best friends. Yet one of my favorite performances was at ten o'clock in the morning, when I played a solo show for a group of senior citizens. It reminded me of the many nights my mom, now deceased, came to the club and was able to enjoy my performances. It is an absolutely wonderful, admirable, and generous thing for a writers' club and the artists and others who benefit from it to have an opportunity to perform in a setting that is so perfectly conducive to making great music, that is, great sound and an intimate feeling, and give our senior citizens who cannot see a show at night a way to feel connected to music created where they live and a sense that they aren't missing anything. It was by far the most memorable time I've had at the club, and if I'd never had any of the others I would love the Bluebird just for that. So thanks, Amy Kurland, for being sensitive and generous to all the community. With an attitude like yours, I'm sure the club will live on and prosper as long as you want it to.

■ ■ ■ ■ ■

Henry Gross was a member of Sha Na Na before breaking away to become a hit-making solo artist. During the heyday of disco, his single "Shannon" was an oasis of Beach Boys–inspired harmonies and hooks.

FOR THE
BENEFIT OF . . .

The Bluebird and benefits have been inseparable since our first year. It was a benefit for World Hunger Relief in 1982 that was also our very first Writers' Night. Money was raised for those who desperately needed it, and a format was begun at the Bluebird that would make us world-famous. It's true: the more you give, the more you get.

Every year we celebrate our anniversary and Christmas with benefits for the Community Resource Center and St. Patrick's Homeless Shelter, respectively. Jay Patten and his band have played every single one of them. Salud! Many of our favorite artists have generously given their time each year to make these benefits our most star-studded affairs.

In 1994 we began what has become another long-running benefit series. Spanning the entire month of January

Steve Seskin and Amy discussing their favorite ways to give blood for the Red Cross.

each year, the Alive Hospice benefit "Friends for Life" has raised oodles of money and resulted in two live CD's taken from the shows.

Bob Cheevers

In 1989 I met a very extraordinary woman. One of the many reasons I admired her was because the skills and sensitivity with which she did her job had such an impact on my life. My best friend was dying of cancer, and she was his hospice nurse. Part of her job was to teach me how to be his caregiver and show me how to help him die at home as comfortably as possible. During his dying process, she and I fell in love, and later we married. We moved to Nashville in 1991, and she went to work for Alive Hospice of Nashville. In 1993 I was asked by the folks she worked with to put together a benefit drawing from the pool of my many talented writer/performer friends.

The following January, the first Alive Hospice Bluebird Benefit Series began. It was a who's who of the Nashville writer/performer world, and the shows spanned the entire month. The first year was a nightmare of balancing schedules and assembling shows that were as diverse as they were interesting. The second year was much easier, and I discovered people were coming to me wanting to be part of the series. After several years the shows nearly assembled themselves due to the stature the series gained and the support that giving to the hospice cause generated in the hearts of the participants. We decided after the third year to put together a cream-of-the-crop CD of live performances, which would then be sold at shows in the coming years. My job was to sort through every song played at every performance and choose the best fifteen. The following year we did a second CD. Both of them sold out and, like the yearly shows, became magic moments of time where the hearts and art of the participants came together in support of a worthy cause. Thanks to the wonderful writer/artist community of Nashville, the turn-of-the-century shows marked the seventh year of the Alive Hospice Benefit Series, making it the one of most successful and longest-running yearly events in the Bluebird's history.

■　■　■　■　■

Bob Cheevers was an original member of the Peppermint Trolley Company. As a writer for television, he won eight regional Emmys in California. Most recently he released several critically acclaimed albums full of songs detailing life along the Mississippi.

Aashid Himmons puts a global spin on things at the First Amendment show.

Over the years we've had the pleasure of raising money and awareness for a diverse list of organizations. Virtually all of them are in the business of helping people in some way, be it physically, mentally, emotionally, financially, or spiritually. That list includes High Hopes, the Peace Action Committee, Youth Alive and Free (Alcohol and Drug Council of Middle Tennessee), Nashville Cares, the Montessori School, Crisis Intervention, the First Amendment Center at Vanderbilt University, and so many more. It's not a tough job and we're glad to do it.

Rusty Young

I've had a lot of fun nights at the Bluebird. But I always remember the night the Bluebird was hosting a benefit for suicide prevention. In that intimate environment we all got to sing with Michael McDonald, David Park, Victoria Shaw, and Stevie Winwood.

Where else but the Bluebird?

■　■　■　■　■

Rusty Young is a founding member of Poco and penned its most famous hit, "Crazy Love." He's a multiinstrumentalist, formed the group Sky Kings with former New Grass Revival bassist John Cowan, and also wrote the hit "Call It Love."

Billy Kirsch

The Bluebird Cafe is a place where songwriters are king and queen. As such we can exert a little influence we wouldn't ordinarily have. The many fund-raiser Writers Nights at the Bluebird represent a special way writers can help influence our world a little bit. My favorite night at the Bluebird was a round I did with Allen Shamblin, Marcus Hummon, and Tom Douglas. It was a benefit for Gilda's Club, a cancer-support community. My wife is a cancer survivor, and the evening was meaningful and emotional for us as well as the many people affected by cancer who came out to support us.

■　■　■　■　■

Kirsch's tender ballad "Holes in the Floor of Heaven" was named one of the Most Performed Songs of 98/99 by BMI. He's also penned "Is It Over Yet" and "Some Rainy Day" for Wynonna as well as the Doug Stone smash "Sometimes I Forget."

Ken Paulson

James Madison would have loved the Bluebird. The author of the First Amendment would have appreciated the steady flow of food, drink, and free expression. He would have embraced a place where songwriters sing what they feel and say what they think.

Not everyone is as receptive to free speech as James Madison was. Music censorship in America goes back more than 260 years. The past forty-five have been a particularly busy time for those who would censor provocative lyrics and

Members of Nashville's rock and rap group Stone Deep kick out the jams at our First Amendment concert.

content. At the First Amendment Center at Vanderbilt University, we strive to help preserve and protect the First Amendment by reminding all Americans of the value of our most fundamental freedoms. That's why we asked Amy Kurland if she would host a festival of free speech at the Bluebird, two nights of music celebrating songs that were censored by government or radio, as well as pop and folk anthems that addressed the issues of our time.

Amy didn't hesitate. She jumped in enthusiastically, providing both energy and good counsel as we developed "Freedom Sings." On

July 13, 1999, it all came together, kicking off with Tommy Womack's take on "Power to the People." Bill Lloyd signed on as musical director and helped put together a two-night line-up of artists with talent, integrity, and a commitment to freedom of expression: Rodney Crowell, John Kay, Beth Nielsen Chapman, Kevin Welch, Jonell Mosser, Radney Foster, Kim Richey,

Rodney Crowell, Kevin Welch, Rodney Harrington, and Radney Foster raise their voices at the First Amendment concert.

Chip Taylor, Robert Earl Keen, Don Henry, Greg Trooper, Robbie Fulks, Tammy Rogers, Stone Deep, Bobby Bare Jr., Dan Baird, Aashid Himmons, Jim Counter, and Rodney Hayden.

"Freedom Sings" gave us two nights of rock, folk, pop, and passion. From Kay's "The Pusher" to Mosser's "Annie Had a Baby"; from Nielsen Chapman's "Society's Child" to Robbie Fulks's gender-bending "The Pill"; from Welch's "Living in the Wasteland" to a group finale of "Give Peace a Chance," we heard firsthand how much music can matter.

Kim Richey may have captured the spirit of the evening best. She chose to perform "Beautiful Fool," Don Henry's touching tribute to Martin Luther King, Jr. "The fella it's about—he wasn't banned. He was murdered for his views and the things he said. But that's the great thing about words and music and everything," said Richey. "Once they're out there, you can't stop them because other people will hear them and repeat them. You can stop the person, but you can't stop the words."

■　■　■　■　■

Ken Paulson is executive director of the First Amendment Center for Free Speech. He's a former newspaper journalist, a new friend of Amy's, and an avid fan of the Bluebird Cafe.

CHAPTER 6
DO I LOOK LIKE I WORK HERE?

When it comes to their employees, bars and restaurants in general are magnets for, shall we say, more colorful types. The Bluebird is no exception, but we wouldn't have it any other way. Over the years we've seen many young men and women join our crew for a little while and then have had the pleasure of watching them soar to new heights, follow their dreams, and do the things they've always wanted to do. We hate to see them go, but we love to see what they do next. One of the things

Kim Richey (with pal Bill Lloyd) cooked up some dishes at the 'Bird before cooking up a zillion hits.

that ties our employees together, besides a love of music, is attitude. Not necessarily a bad attitude, just attitude. If we've never won any awards for service, well, we're willing to bet we've had some of the more memorable waiters, bartenders, kitchen and office staff in the biz. And they have some great memories of their own.

THE KITCHEN STAFF

Or, Big Hearts and Small Kitchens

Before he wrote the John Michael Montgomery smash "Friends," Jerry Holland was a friend to our dishes.

You may not see them, but they're definitely aware of you and what's going on onstage. The guys and gals who've worked in the kitchen at the Bluebird share a camaraderie not unlike that among those who've been in battle together. With the waitresses screaming at them for their order while they bump into each other in a kitchen not much bigger than a foxhole, it's easy to see why.

Mark D. Benner

It must have been around 1984, and I was only doing the desserts and occasionally barbacking while attending college full time. I was working on a wood carving in the sculpture department at Tennessee State University with my friend Mic (pronounced "Mike") West when I foolishly shoved the large wood chisel I was using into my hand, creating a sizable wound that immediately began gushing blood. Mic almost passed out, but I was able to persuade him to drive me to a hospital. It turned out Mic didn't drive. He was from Los Angeles and had never bothered to learn, so I ended up giving him driving lessons on the way. They patched me up, and when I was finished, neither of us wanted to go back and work on sculpture, so I invited Mic to go to the Bluebird for a drink.

It was a slow night at the club, two or three guys sitting around playing acoustic guitars, singing, and not much of a crowd. Mic and I sat at the bar, had a couple of old Bushmills, and proceeded to talk. Back in those days the club wasn't totally given over to the listening-room atmosphere it has today—in fact, most acts were bands and played pretty loud. One could usually carry on a conversation without

Mark Benner and his friend Melissa at an early New Year's party.

disrupting the performance. I had been given some pain pills for my hand, and with the alcohol and the usual loud and jovial conversations Mic and I had, we became too loud. We weren't aware of our rudeness. We were shushed several times, and I'm sure we must have been the first ever to be given the Bluebird *shhh,* even though it took several years before it became the official mantra.

Finally Amy came over and coaxed us back into the kitchen, where we were allowed to carry on with our merrymaking but had to be shushed several more times. Amy was concerned about how we were getting home and also was pretty anxious to get us out of the club. She ended up driving Mic and me back over to TSU to let Mic off. She brought me back to the club, but the music was over and I went home. Yes, I'm almost sure that, even though Amy doesn't realize it, that was the first official Bluebird *shhh.*

■ ■ ■ ■ ■ ■

Mark Benner worked with Amy in her first culinary endeavor: selling quiche and Italian ices from a pushcart in downtown Nashville. He went on to become the Bluebird's first chef. He's a potter and community organizer and now works as a schoolteacher in a small town in Colorado. This book was his idea.

David Billings

As my mind wanders back to 1984, I think not of Big Brother but rather of the infamous Bluebird Cafe. I was seventeen years old, and the world through my eyes was a strange and welcoming place. I ended up working at the Bluebird after a stint at Ruby Tuesday's. My interview lasted all of five minutes, and soon I was part of what has become a family of fond memories to me. For those of you who have only recently come to know the Bluebird, I will go over some brief history, a tale of a game room gone global.

In 1984 I was hired (sorry about the Dickensesque start) and loved the job from the beginning. A restaurant is the only place where you can take people from all walks of life, give them jobs, and have them turn into family. And what a family I walked into that year. Amy Kurland had on staff two of the most inspirational yet bizarre chefs I have ever worked with, Don James and Mark Benner. Also a strange lunch crew—yes, we did serve lunch once upon a nightmare—that was more like a family that had gone union rather than a crew of individuals. Then there were the night servers, who were my sounding board for my early trials and tribulations in flirtation, a bartender notorious for losing his glasses in the ice machine, and of course the endless stream of performers, both great and—well, let's just say, less than great. I recall many names that have become obscure, and many names that still linger. There is a secret I must pass on to all readers. During Amy's attempts to maintain a crew, she hired one aspiring musician, name not disclosed to protect the bizarre. He convinced Amy that he needed a couple of hibachi grills to do the cuisine he had in mind.

And moments later, he only had nine digits left. Not really—"Danger" David Billings is a professional chef.

After each night he would put them on the back porch to cool. Somehow this writer of the single "Damn Those Memories" cut halfway through his Achilles tendon on the edge of one of those small grills. Thus starting my lifelong rule of no dancing in the kitchen. The story continues with his departure from the restaurant, and in our fixing a hole that used to be in the back hall. Yes, entombed in the infamous Bluebird Cafe is one hibachi, which someday may be uncovered by Geraldo Rivera . . .

■   ■   ■   ■   ■

One of our more famous chefs, Dave Billings went on to work in many restaurants in Tennessee. He's now sous chef at a prestigious bistro in Windsor, California.

Bernie Pittman

One day while cleaning the ladies' bathroom at the Bluebird Cafe, I walked in on a sight that I will have in my "rep" of celebrity sightings forever. John Frogge and myself were working together at the time, in the kitchen as well as the entire restaurant. We switched off, so that one day I would work in the kitchen and the next day I would work cleaning the restaurant. It was my day to clean the night Melissa Etheridge was to play and she was there doing a sound check. She wasn't very well known then, but like many people who play at the Bluebird, she soon after became very famous. Anyway, when cleaning the bathrooms, the first thing you always did was open the door and hold it open by placing the garbage can in front of it. So, when I entered the women's bathroom, Melissa Etheridge was standing in front of the toilet pulling up her pants. Needless to say, I was shocked, not only had I entered the ladies' room without knocking, I had also seen the half-clothed stud in all of her glory. For a seventeen-year-old farm boy, this was quite a sight. Fortunately for me, she was quite a sport and dis-missed the incident with a small laugh. And even more fortunately for me, I have the memory of being a small handful of men who have ever seen the star partially clothed.

Our little Bernie Pittman looking a lot more sweet and innocent than he really is.

■ ■ ■ ■ ■

These days you'll find Bernie working in some of the finest bistros and restaurants in New York City. But before he moved to the Big Apple and attended one of the city's finest culinary institutes, he was just our little Bernie, making a club sandwich in the Bluebird kitchen.

Tony Woodruff

I started off at the Bluebird Cafe as a barback many years ago. Katy McCoy and Jennifer Barnette were the main bartenders back then. It was during this time that I saw one of the most hilarious things ever at the club.

Tony Woodruff isn't French but he still looks good in a beret.

Jennifer was tending bar on a Don Schlitz night. The show was onstage, and this sets the whole thing up, because that meant the entire audience had its back to the bartender. As many people already know, Don is a fun-loving guy, but his song set is quite sensitive. So, the audience was completely focused on Don.

Now, Jennifer is a lovely lady with a very voluptuous body. She went to the bathroom about halfway through the show and readied herself. During one of Don's more touching songs, Jennifer flashes him her breasts, which are covered with two smiley faces. This floors Don. He's laughing so hard it stops the show for at least five minutes. No one in the room except for Don, Jennifer, the waitresses, and myself know why he's completely lost it.

Who says we can't loosen up at the Bluebird?

■　■　■　■　■

Tony Woodruff is one of the rare Bluebird employees who doesn't write songs. An avid music lover, poker player, and whiffle-ball enthusiast, he hails from Dalton, Georgia.

Bobby Ross

I came to Nashville with a ten-dollar bill, an old guitar, one suitcase filled halfway with my writing and the other half with my cooking costumes. I was going to make it or break it in the music business. And I could cook, so I didn't have to worry about starving or any of that artistic stuff. When I first got to Music Row I fell in love with it, and I've lived here ever since. One of the first places people here I was meeting told me I had to go to was the Bluebird Cafe. Now, I reckon I should tell ya, I'm from out West. Out there, when I was growing up in the bars and "rough and ready" rooms where early rock and roll and country music was playing, people mostly talked and yelled and acted drunk.

When I actually moved away from the jukebox and onto the stage and started making my living playing live music, it was still the same ol' thing. We were just background noise so the folks could drink and make general fools of themselves. Now, I ain't sayin' that was bad. No, that was just the way it was. And I still liked playing music! But when I first walked into the Bluebird, after having stood in line for a spell, well, I walked into paradise.

That night, with the crowd occupying every single chair and bar stool and standing, I got my first glimpse of Amy. Amy Kurland, that is. The lights went way down except for this one shining on Amy, and the crowd was talking. That's right, talking! Amy stood there, very stern. Much the same as one of those schoolteachers you would have imagined out in the West back in the cowboy

Chef Bobby Ross giving his standard response to complaints.

days. Slowly, the talking stopped. Amy folded her arms as if she was very disgusted with us. (Of course, I was speechless.) After a bit more time passed, the place was very quiet. Amy began speaking into the microphone, very, very softly, but her words carried. She scolded the audience. She mildly explained, in a very firm manner, that when you are in her establishment, the Bluebird Cafe, you will listen to the songwriter. That is because they have spent countless hours shedding sweat and blood to perform their songs for this audience, and this audience will give them the courtesy of listening. Then she walked off the stage, and the show began. Amy Kurland, that's why I love the Bluebird Cafe.

■ ■ ■ ■ ■

Bobby Ross was a Bluebird chef and definitely one of our most colorful employees. A veteran of the Vietnam War, he has spent much of his time organizing events to honor and benefit other vets.

Elliott Duke

I have so many stories about the Bluebird Cafe that it's hard to pick one for inclusion in this book. I could tell you about the day vocal overdubs were cut for a Steve Forbert record. I could tell you about having the opportunity to hear Ramblin' Jack Elliott reminiscing about a cross-country odyssey. I could tell you about meeting Lauren Bacall, but I will save those stories for another time.

The Confidence in Public Speaking courses were not entirely successful for Elliott Duke.

The Bluebird Cafe has become one of the premier clubs in the country for songwriters. The In the Round format has proven an effective way to hear what's happening on Music Row. Sadly, much of this music is forced to adhere to the tight constraints of commercial radio or the bottom-line expectations of a record company. However, there are nights at the Bluebird where you are able to hear a songwriter who is not afraid to paint outside the lines. Songwriters who step onstage and help define the times we live in and are able to inspire—the ultimate goal of all art. I like to think that T-Bone Burnett recognized this when he wrote:

There are those who play for money, babe
There are those who play for fame
There are still those who only play
For the love of the game.

So, ultimately this story is about the artists I've seen at the Bluebird who play for the love of the game.

- MOSE ALLISON
- DAVE ALVIN
- PAUL BRADY
- JUNIOR BROWN
- RICHARD BUCKNER
- T-BONE BURNETT
- PETER CASE
- GUY CLARK
- IRIS DEMENT
- STEVE EARLE
- RAMBLIN' JACK ELLIOTT
- JOE ELY
- ALEJANDRO ESCOVEDO
- STEVE FORBERT
- MARK GERMINO

- NANCI GRIFFITH
- TOM T. HALL
- JOHN WESLEY HARDING
- EMMYLOU HARRIS
- TED HAWKINS
- MARK KNOPFLER
- KRIS KRISTOFFERSON
- JAMES MCMURTRY
- BUDDY AND JULIE MILLER
- BILL MONROE
- GEOFF MULDAUR
- MICKEY NEWBERRY
- BOB NEUWIRTH
- TIM O'BRIEN
- DAVE OLNEY
- JOHN PRINE
- DARRELL SCOTT
- RON SEXSMITH
- BILLY JOE SHAVER
- CHRIS SMITHER
- TOWNES VAN ZANDT
- GILLIAN WELCH AND DAVID RAWLINGS
- LUCINDA WILLIAMS

Emmylou Harris and Lucinda Williams together on our little stage. 'Nuff said.

It was an incredibly special night when Grandpa Jones and John Hartford did a round with Bill Monroe.

■ ■ ■ ■ ■

One of our most loyal employees, Elliott Duke is our resident Bob Dylan freak and restaurant day manager. He came to Nashville and the Bluebird after attending college at East Tennessee State University in Johnson City and working at the now defunct Ella Guru's. It's probably safe to say Elliott has the largest collection of Dylan bootlegs in the state of Tennessee.

Erika Wollam Nichols

My memories of the Bluebird through all these years are really a series of memories. . . . Working lunches during the year of the locusts and having both Chet Atkins and Minnie Pearl come in screaming with locusts on their clothing. Mark Knopfler coming in for lunch with Chet Atkins and all of us hiding behind the bar to see them. Gary Bussey yelling at me for not running him a tab without a credit card. Billy Gibbons ordering a Bud, telling me I had a nice smile, and tipping me five dollars. Designing a flyer for Mose Allison and having him autograph it. Interviewing Don Schlitz for a journalism class assignment. Dressing up as an elf with Liz Hengber in hopes of getting extra tips during the holiday season. Tears springing to my eyes as Bobby Braddock sang "He Stopped Loving Her Today." Singing a cappella on my last night ('88) and having Jonell Mosser and Harlan Howard tell me I sounded good. Using the Bluebird as the subject for a PR plan and creating a survey that led to starting the Early Shows. The night there were thirty people in the room, Billy Prine was onstage singing about Christmas in Chicago, and he was joined by brother John and someone at one of my tables asked incredulously, "Is that *John* Prine?" I'll never forget the look on his face. The chance to meet so many of my heroes at the bar: Guy Clark, John Prine, Peter Case, Dan Bern, James McMurtry, to sit on the credenza and see others: Maria Muldaur, Steven Bruton, Mary Chapin Carpenter; and to discover others. So many people have given their souls to writing and playing the music that keeps the rest of us going.

The all-time best moment was the night in June 1989 when T-Bone Burnett was scheduled to play at the club, and Amy, knowing I am a huge fan, asked if I would go and pick him up at the Hermitage Hotel. When I arrived, he came down on the elevator and asked if I minded having a cup of tea before we left. We rode back up to his suite where he ordered the tea, sat down, picked up his guitar, and played one Hank Williams song after another. Time stopped and although the show later was marvelous, I'll never forget what it felt like to sit in that hotel room listening to "Your Cheatin' Heart" on a summer night in Nashville.

■　■　■　■　■

Erika Wollam Nichols started working at the Bluebird in 1984 as a lunch waitress when she came to Nashville from Massachusetts. Over the years she worked as waitress, hostess, bookeeper, and bartender; booked talent; and designed flyers. She officially left in 1988, came back in 1991, left again, and came back again until 1996. She is now vice president of marketing at the new Country Music Hall of Fame but she'd probably still be subbing behind the bar if she got her ABC card renewed!

Bryan Hartman

A few years back, we had a wide assortment of intellectually challenged waitresses who did not seem to grasp the notion that when I closed the kitchen for the night, it meant that the kitchen was closed, period! No more fries, no more pies, and no more latecomers! Well, one night about ten-twenty, Olivia Newton-John walked in (SANDY!). Unfortunately for her, I had shut the kitchen down twenty minutes before (we're talkin' lights off, I'm clockin' out, and I'm goin' home). Even though one of our lovely waitresses practically begged me to make Olivia an order of fries, I, in so many words, re-

Bartender Keith Lamb and chef Brian Hartman model the latest in headwear for the sharp-dressed food service person.

minded her that McDonald's was still open and that the only grease Olivia was gonna see from me was my bad Rizzo impersonation.

■　■　■　■　■

Brian Hartman has been our chef for over two years. He's also a fine drummer and perhaps the world's biggest Kiss fan. Somehow, he also finds time to attend Belmont College, where he's enrolled in the music-business program. He doesn't make a habit of snubbing celebrities.

THE BAR STAFF

Or, I Don't Care Who You Are, Get Outta My Way

Stretch

I used to cocktail waitress at the Bluebird. It's not like it is now, with the *shhhh* and all that. We had some pretty loud and wild nights. I remember one night the Billy Stone Band was playing. They were a real redneck band, and they used to bring all their redneck friends with them. We always knew that it was going to be wild and rough when they were going to play. They had this one guy who did the door for them, called Poohbah. I always thought they were calling him Pool Ball, but I found out later it was Poohbah. Poohbah was really big, and they used to call him the Grand Poobah. The Billy Stone Band liked to drink really cheap whisky, and to keep from having to buy drinks from the waitress or the bar they would sneak their own bottle in. It was Poohbah's job to hide the liquor. He would keep it behind the little waitress stand, and the guys in the band would go over to the stand in front of the door and Poohbah would pour some whisky into their cups, keeping it hidden from the staff. Usually it was Kessler's or something cheaper, if there is anything cheaper.

Anyway, the band had started playing and the kitchen had just finished the Black Forest cakes. The cook had brought them out and they were sitting on the hutch waiting to be placed in the dessert case, which back then was near the front door.

I was trying to keep an eye on the cakes but got busy and when I was able to get back to the front I saw that one of them was gone. I looked around and saw Poohbah sort of waddling like a duck out the front door, looking very suspicious. So I followed him out to the sidewalk, and he was still taking little baby steps and using his body to hide the cake in front of him. He put the cake on the hood of a car parked in front and started eating some with his fingers. His back was still turned, and so I walked up pretty close and said, "Pool Ball, What are you doing?" in a very intimidating tone. He jumped, nearly knocking the cake onto the ground. I said, "Where'd you get that cake?" He was pretty much speechless, and I told him he was going to have to pay for it. He said he'd give it back, and I said, "Not after you've had your grubby paws all over it!"

Poohbah had to pay twenty-two dollars for the cake. Then after he'd paid the full amount he sat at the waitress station and ate the whole thing. I'm sure he had some of the whisky along with it.

■　■　■　■　■

Stretch, whose real name is Deborah McEuen, was with us in our earliest days. She went to waitress at the Sportsman's Grill and was named Best Waitress by the Nashville Scene.

Liz Hengber

When I was a waitress at the Bluebird Cafe I met many singers I had admired over the years, but meeting Janis Ian was absolutely the greatest for me. The reason goes back to high school. When I was seventeen I lost the student-council election to Lori Lebowitz. Not only did I lose, it was a freakin' landslide for Lori. I think some tough kids in my homeroom voted for me 'cause I promised a smoking lounge. Other than that, I was history. Anyway, that night I listened to Janis Ian's "At Seventeen" over and over. I will never forget how it got me past the total humiliation.

So years later there I am taking Janis Ian's order at the Bluebird Cafe. I of course related the entire story to her. She was great. She listened, laughed, and was grateful that her song touched my life. Out of all the stars I had met at this cafe, she was without a doubt the most gracious. At the end of the night I went to clean up my tables. Where Janis was sitting there was a tip waiting for me. It was one hundred dollars.

■   ■   ■   ■

Before becoming a hit songwriter, Liz Hengber was a waitress at the Bluebird Cafe. Her credits include three smash hits for Reba McEntire, "For My Broken Heart," "And Still," and "It's Your Call," as well as "Unconditional" by Clay Davidson and "She Can't Save Him" by Lisa Brokop.

Barbara Cloyd

Hosting the Monday-night Open Mic is one of the best things in my life. I feel like a part of Nashville's musical history. Almost every writer who's new in town comes there, and I get to see them all. David Wilcox and Garth Brooks impressed me immediately. Kenny Chesney didn't, but he sure does now. Brett Jones, Chuck Cannon, Tim Johnson, and Steve Leslie were all regulars before they hit it big as writers. The over-

Barbara Cloyd performing her Lorrie Morgan hit "I Guess You Had to Be There."

whelming majority of the ones I see will never have success, but human souls have such a need to express themselves and it's important that they have a place to do it. After twelve years I still have moments of being amazed by how beautiful it is, even when the songs aren't.

■   ■   ■   ■   ■

Barbara Cloyd has been the host of our Monday-night Open Mic for over ten years. Her dedication as a songwriter finally paid off when Lorrie Morgan recorded "I Guess You Had to Be There."

Katy McCoy

Having worked at the Bluebird for ten years, I find it hard to narrow down all the wonderful experiences to one or two. There is a magic

that happens in this little club that is unlike anything else I've ever felt. It's when a songwriter or a group of songwriters are performing and the entire audience is glued to their seats. The electricity runs through the air, and everything else in life is forgotten as the songwriter and audience share the experience. The amazing thing is that this intense experience happens at least once a week. I had so many wonderful firsts:

Katy McCoy was a Bluebird institution for over a decade.

serving sodas to Garth Brooks and his wife the night he made his debut performance for all of the labels before he was signed, watching Nanci Griffith mesmerize her audience to the point that no one moved a muscle for hours. Waiting on Johnny and June Cash was a total thrill, and of course there was the night the lights went out in Nashville and Kevin Welch and his band gave a beautiful acoustic, candlelit performance.

But there is one night that stands out in my mind because it was one of those moments when the songwriter bares his soul and the magic is shared among the room. It was a Sunday Writers Night, and the special guest was Jon Vezner. Jon introduced a new song that he and Don Henry had just written. The song, "Where You've Been," was recorded later by his wife, Kathy Mattea. Written for his grandparents, it tells a beautiful true love story, and the room was hanging intently on to every word. As he finished the last verse there was a little choke in his voice and a tear slipped down his cheek. The entire room broke into tears. The soundman was crying, I was crying, the cook was crying. It was such a personal moment of sharing, and that is what I love about the songwriter, the music, and the Bluebird Cafe. Thanks, Amy.

Katy McCoy was one of our longest-lasting employees. First as a waitress and later as bar manager, Katy was a Bluebird institution. She currently resides in New Mexico and was recently married.

Mark Irwin

I went to the Bluebird my first night in Nashville. Besides being blown away by the performer (Fred Knobloch), I was so taken with the place that I started working there the next day. And I stayed for six years. Their obvious devotion to songwriters (both newcomers and old-timers) made me feel very much at home, and in turn helped me to become a more supportive person as well.

It was the perfect place for me because being inundated with so much great music night after night truly helped me become a better songwriter. And I developed relationships that are still going strong today. I've had so many memorable experiences there that it would be impossible to choose just one that made a lasting impression. I could talk about the time I tried to impress Don Schlitz (whom I didn't know then) with my plans to take over the town with my music—only to be humbled when he got up onstage.

I could talk about the first time I heard Tony Arata and how inspiring it was. I could talk about the countless Monday nights listening to the music of and getting to hang out with Mike Henderson, first with his band the Kingsnakes and then with the Bluebloods. Getting to see such a dynamic performer grow and grow week after week was truly a joyful experience for me.

Or I could talk about the time I stayed up all night with the Indigo Girls after one of their performances just talking about music (and drinking of course—sorry, Amy). Or how privileged I felt to hear artists like Chris Isaak and Melissa Etheridge and even Garth

Mark "Bubba" Irwin with a grin that only a number one hit can bring.

Brooks, Trisha Yearwood, and Vince Gill before the rest of the world really knew who they were. Or I could talk about how the Bluebird was responsible for introducing me to the music of Mark Germino

99

At the close of his set during the 1990 NEA Extravaganza, Mark Germino did this to his guitar. While we would never condone such a thing, Amy did think it would make some fine wall art for the club.

and eventually the man himself, who has become for me a benchmark of sorts for brilliance in writing and in life.

But mostly I guess I would have to talk about all the friendships and cowriting relationships that have developed strictly because of the Bluebird.

I know my experience was a unique one, and I owe a huge debt to Amy and the club. Mostly for realizing the specialness of songs and their writers, but also for their influence on me not only as a songwriter but as a human being as well.

Oh, yeah, there was that time when Tanya Tucker pinched my cheek in the kitchen, but I guess I'll save that story for a different book.

■ ■ ■ ■ ■

Mark Irwin is one of our favorite Bluebird success stories. While a bartender at the Bluebird he wrote "Here in the Real World" with Alan Jackson. It launched Jackson's career as an artist and Mark's career as a professional songwriter.

Sam Russell

We sell about a thousand T-shirts a year. That's Amy, Don Schlitz, Sam Russell, and Jon Ims doing the supermodel thing.

Yes, it's true. I was a bartender at the Bluebird Cafe in the mid-nineties. A California transplant, I had always made my living on the other side of the bar, playing in bands, trios, duos, and, for a few too many years, as a solo act.

Anyway, I had been at the 'Bird (that's what we "insiders" call it) a couple of years and had waited on one particular songwriter—a very successful songwriter—countless times. He was playing the club two to three times a month, yet he never engaged me in any fashion other than to order something from the bar. He never called me by name because he didn't know it or couldn't remember it. Having played clubs myself, I could understand how one might play a bar a few times and not remember employees' names or even care. This, however, had been going on for at least two years, and he did seem to commit to memory the names of all the cocktail waitresses. By the way, it should be noted, this guy never tipped.

Finally, one night he comes to the bar to order something and I decide enough is enough. It was about to become simply rude. So I looked him in the eye and said, "Dick" (not his real name but kind of appropriate), "what's my name?" He got a lost sort of look in his eye, thought for a minute, and said, "Honey?"

Sam Russell's Hollywood double fooled no one.

I still don't think he knows my name, or cares, but with a comeback like that you gotta give the guy some slack.

■　■　■　■　■

Sam Russell was a Bluebird bartender for several years and can still be found performing at the club, either with his band or with his "Studs on a Budget" round. He's a native of Southern California, where he cut his teeth playing the clubs between L.A. and Tahoe.

John Mark Higginbotham

A few years back Gary Burr and Co. decided to throw a pajama birthday party in Gary's honor, which wasn't all that unusual except for the fact that it was an unseasonably cold night.

If anyone has been here in the last few years, they know the procedure of lining up people with reservations to one side of the door and standers on the other. This was my idea, however, we hadn't yet established a time for cutting off admission at the door. Therefore, there was often a mix of early- and late-show patrons in the club by 8:00 P.M. We didn't create new policies like ending admission thirty minutes before the end of the early show and others until later, as a result of the growing pains attributed to the recently filmed movie *The Thing Called Love*.

On this night the patrons of the early show couldn't help but notice the slow but sure influx of inappropriately attired people with reservations for the late show. And the contrast became blatantly evident when the forever loved and much missed Mama Price strolled in sporting the latest in Mama Price–sized bathrobes, wearing curlers, a shower cap, and a face full of cold cream. It almost literally *stopped* the show.

It was then that I decided to cut off admission for the early show, but there was soon a horde of, shall we say, casually underdressed people lined up outside the Bluebird shivering. By this time, some of the early-show people, even some vacationers, had realized that something pleasurably amiss was about to happen and they had left the club, gone to their homes or hotels, changed, and were back ready to attend the coming function in all their underclothed splendor. It was a zoo. And, for all of those who were there, an unforgettable Bluebird moment.

∎　∎　∎　∎　∎

John Mark has worked off and on as a Bluebird host for nearly ten years. One of our friendliest employees, he came to Nashville from Texas.

THE OFFICE STAFF

Two Phone Lines, Two Thousand Requests

Nannette Clark

Although we did not meet at the Bluebird, my husband, Brett Clark, was the first dishwasher and was there for opening night.

I have fond memories of the In the Dark Shows, which were during the power outage from the ice storms of 1994, I believe. These shows were unplugged, needless to say, and the only lighting was candles. The ambiance was incredible, with Kevin Welch singing his story songs. The show must go on. I remember hearing Tony Arata sing "The Dance" before Garth Brooks made it a classic.

Nannette Clark and hubby Breet obviously enjoyed the "refreshments" at the staff Christmas party.

I remember all of the last-minute special requests that came in from celebrities (and those who thought they were) for a sold-out show. We always tried to be accommodating, but never at the expense of patrons who were already seated or had reservations. I always considered it a challenge to squeeze in that extra table to seat those special guests. I particularly remember the night that Lauren Bacall, who was a childhood idol of mine, came in. She was so gracious and classy. I even sold her and Peter Jennings a CD of the artist playing that night.

The Debutantes in the Round with Pam Tillis, Ashley Cleveland, Tricia Walker, and Karen Staley was a hoot. They wore prom dresses. I remember asking Walter Hyatt to play on so many early shows and, later on, late shows, and how shocked and saddened I was to learn his plane went down in the Florida Everglades.

I had an incredible time working at the Bluebird with all the wonderful folks. It was an experience that I wouldn't have missed for the world. Thanks!

■　　■　　■　　■　　■

Nannette Clark worked at the Bluebird both as a doorperson and a booker while attending law school. Now married with children, she works in the area of child advocacy.

Fran Overall

One of the most fun times at the Blue-bird was being around for one of Gary Burr's pajama parties for his birthday. Gary wore a blue print number with matching bag and shoes. Russell Smith had on tight red farmer Johns with cowboy attire. Bob DiPiero had on a pink-and-yellow Tweety Bird outfit. Jim Photoglo had on slinky black pajamas. Half the audience wore pajamas, robes, and house shoes and brought stuffed animals. Hey, any excuse to

Famed producer T-Bone Burnette backing a particularly hairy Rodney Crowell.

dress up and be crazy! The music and stories were great, of course. And chocolate birthday cake for everyone. It made my birthday week-end.

The other favorite memory was sitting ringside for Carole King,

Gary Burr, Matraca Berg, and Rodney Crowell. Such a special night. When Carole was playing her first song, I realized that *Tapestry* had been my first eight-track tape!

■　■　■　■　■

Fran is a Tennessee native with a B.S. in recording-industry management as well as an M.A. in clinical psychology from Middle Tennessee State University. At the Bluebird she handles the gathering of publishing information for TV shows and CD releases, and oversees reservations. She's also a Jimmy Buffett fan, a.k.a., a Parrothead.

Suzanne Spooner

During my time here at the Bluebird I have been witness to many amazing and surprising events, one of which occurred on Halloween 1998. My friend Teresa and I had spent all night at a Halloween costume party in Belle Meade. She went as a doctor, and I went as a country girl. I had on my gingham shirt, overalls, pigtails with bows and all. After we left the party we decided to run by the Bluebird to say hi and show off our creative costumes.

We went in the back door and heard this voice that sounded kind of familiar. Danny Flowers, Russell Smith, and Jim Photoglo were all slated to play, but this voice didn't sound like any of them. I walked in and looked at the round, and there sat Vince Gill belting out one of his songs. I had only been working here for five months, and this was the first time anyone "famous" had come in unannounced.

There I sat at the bar in my country-girl getup, with Teresa in her doctor garb. And no one else was dressed up at all. Talk about a happy Halloween. It's one I'll never forget.

■　■　■　■　■

Suzanne Spooner was events manager at the Bluebird. She grew up in Quincy, Florida, and attended Wesleyan College in Macon, Georgia. When she's not in the Bluebird offices with her ear glued to the phone, she dabbles in her other vocation: "baby-sitter extraordinaire."

AND THEN THERE'S THIS GUY...

We don't really have a classification for this guy—we're not even sure he's a guy, for that matter. The truth is, no one knows who Blurbman is, we just know he's been writing the blurbs for the Bluebird calendar since Moses rode the river in a basket. Many people have tried to guess his true identity . . . and failed. He's received hate mail and fan letters, and there's even a rumor of a made-for-TV movie about him starring Loni Anderson, Fabio, and Morris the Cat. We can't wait. All we can say is, should anyone unravel the mystery of this guy and happen to pass him on the street, feel free to bop him over the head with a copy of *Totally Gross Jokes Volume 13*.

Blurbman

BLURBMAN REMEMBERS 75 YEARS AT THE BLUEBIRD

Where to start? There are so many memories inside the hallowed walls of the Bluebird Cafe. Blurbman was there at the opening night when Tanya Tucker, Dolly Parton, and Lulu Roman danced naked on the bar. Oh, wait . . . wrong club. Okay, well, Blurbman was there when Garth first walked in. It was I who suggested he lose the mustache, get a bigger hat, and tighten up the jeans. I'm still waiting for some sort of compensation.

Blurbman has been a friend and inspiration to so many of the writers who've become synonymous with the Bluebird. I told Don Schlitz about a gambler I met on a train. I took Thom Schuyler for a ride in my old yellow car. I made many passes at that hunky Bob DiPiero, using my subtle "wink." Beth Nielsen Chapman celebrated my kiss. And it was only after hearing about the Blurbman inflatable dolls that Gary Burr wrote "Sure Love." Obviously my influence is undeniable.

What many people don't know, however, is that the Bluebird was initially opened as an all-male revue. It was to feature Blurbman and the Blurbettes. Zoning laws and a few Green Hills blue-hairs promptly put an end to that, but there are still a few underground videotapes of the shows in circulation. (I'm the one in the leopard-skin thong . . . well, right before Amy rips it off. Oh, those wild early days.)

The years have flown by. Clubs have come and gone. Lawsuits have been settled. Probation is almost over and one thing remains: the Bluebird. Well, Blurbman and the Bluebird. In fact, screw the Bluebird, I'm starting my own club. Hey, Amy, can I borrow some money?

■   ■   ■   ■   ■

If we believed everything Blurbman writes about himself, we'd have to believe he's a cross-dressing redneck with a love of cheap humor, cheap beer, and cheap women, living in a trailer park somewhere near Bucksnort, Tennessee. And he may very well be.

CHAPTER 7

WE OUGHTTA BE IN PICTURES

Or, Yes, Mr. Bogdanovich, We're Ready for Our Close-up

They didn't get it exactly right, but we had a fun time watching them try. *The Thing Called Love* was Hollywood's attempt to get inside the hearts and minds of Nashville's songwriting community and inside the Bluebird Cafe too. Unfortunately, Tinseltown's view of Music City was still mired in the big-hats-and-cowboy-boots frame of mind. There's still a certain element of that in Nashville, but there's so much more to Twang Town than twang.

Sometime in 1992 Amy began to hear rumors about a script floating around, said to be about Nashville and, more specifically, the Bluebird Cafe. It wasn't the first time such rumors had been heard, so she took them with a grain of salt. Finally, it became clear that the ru-

Pat Barber models one of the many big hats the folks in Hollywood still believe the folks in Nashville wear.

The set built in Hollywood to re-create the Bluebird interior. Their chairs are nicer than ours.

Another view of the Hollywood Bluebird.

mors were true, the script was real, and a movie was going to be made. The script was written by an L.A.–based writer, Carol Heikkinen, after she saw the 48 Hours episode about Nashville and the Bluebird. While that episode was informative, it doesn't quite tell the whole story, and consequently, neither did the script. But since the Bluebird was central to so much of the film, Amy was brought on as a consultant and she did her best to convince director, Peter Bogdanovich (The Last Picture Show), and the Hollywood suits that the only people wearing hats in Nashville are the tourists. It didn't work, of course, but what the heck—she got paid.

So Amy and the rest of the staff got a crash course in moviemaking, and the first thing we learned was that it was not nearly as glamorous as one might have thought. There's a lot of "hurry up and wait" involved. The interior of the Bluebird proved to be too small to film in, so a replica was built on a Hollywood soundstage. This meant that Amy got to hang out in the City of Angels for a while and show the folks on the set how to make it all look right and real. As an added bonus, Amy, a diehard Trekkie, got to visit a neighboring set, which was home to Star Trek: The Next Generation.

They did, however, shoot a lot of scenes in the Bluebird parking lot. We got to see River Phoenix, Sandra Bullock, Dermot Mulroney, and Samantha Mathis close up. River was, unfortunately, on the downhill slide that would eventually find him overdosing on an L.A. sidewalk. It's a waste and a loss we still feel. K. T.

Oslin (*80's Ladies*) played the part of Amy, renamed Lucy for the film.

If *The Thing Called Love* wasn't a cinematic classic on a par with *Nashville*, still, the overall experience gave us so many wonderful memories and the kind of exposure a club can only dream of.

Pat Barber

I played a song once and someone clapped, so I had to move to Nashville. I was a stonemason from Aspen. Now I'm a songwriter, and I'm just laying stone until the "mailbox money" starts coming in. You'll never hear the song on the radio—the song that drove me here—because program directors know that drive-time listeners don't want to hear "Tears and Boogars." It got a giggle out of my kids, though.

When I arrived at Music City, I beat on a few doors, suffered some kind rejections, and realized that I'd better dig in for the long haul and get a job. I chose cab driving. I didn't know the city. Cab companies don't require that. I wanted to have a job where I could write songs, play guitar, and get paid for it. So I played between fares. I played the Opry, the Ryman, and other big cabstands. By the time I got my guitar stolen the second time and turned in my keys, I knew my way around Twang Town and had another song that will never get airplay. I played "Dawn on Dickerson Road" for "Lucille" writer Hal Bynum. He set me straight. Radioland doesn't want to hear about a cab-driving tune-smith whose best client is an escort. Makes me wish they had cable ra-dio for songs "too hot for FM, just right for Showtime."

Anyway, they said if you're a songwriter, you have to play the Bluebird. I auditioned on a Sunday, got there late, and parked my cab across the street at H. G. Hills. If you saw the movie *Thing Called Love*, you'd think I was in the Drake Motel lot and that Sandra Bul-lock was living there in a room that looked like a set from *Laugh-In*. I opened the trunk to get the shirt I'd pressed that morning for the Day They Discovered Pat Barber. No bag—it was on the way to Dallas with the last bunch of tourists I dropped at the airport. Not a prob-lem, I just "warshed off" and did the gig in a plain smelling-like-a-cabdriver-wannabe-songwriter shirt.

I was wannabe number 60. That evening *48 Hours* was shooting a documentary on the 'Bird. There were hot lights and cameras all around. They were discovering Marty Brown that day, but they still filmed my audition—just to make me nervous. A rude cameraman squatted down in front of me (really violating my special zone) getting an artistic angle on my demise. I didn't have to wait for the "You're welcome to try again" letter to know that Amy was going to flunk me. Poor girl, she could hardly look at me. I saw the painful embarrassment behind her smile when I finished the one verse and chorus that my future in Music City hinged upon. But, like any self-promoting tunesmith with a naïve belief in his God-given unction to share his gift with the world, I shook it off and was offering a rendition of "Boogars" to a reporter before I left the parking lot.

When Amy found out my day job was masonry, she encouraged me not to quit it just yet and made my summer, sending me to family and friends to do masonry, painting, and handyman things. When she told me that I could do a "real" and be in the movie *Thing Called Love*, (doing a "real" is when you do what you do in real life in a movie), I jumped on the opportunity. Maybe they would ask me to sing "Boogars" or "Turbo," my new and sad little ditty about a kitty that I taught to fetch and then accidentally sucked through my pickup's radiator fan. If you saw the movie, you know how that turned out. Nope, no feline gumbo on the silver screen. Bad taste.

So what if they didn't want my songs. Now I have some name-dropping ammo. "Yes, I've worked with Sandra Bullock. She was relatively unknown then, doing a Peter Bogdanovich movie with Samantha Mathis and River Phoenix (his last, by the way). What was Sandra like? Oh, I thought that she mustn't be that big because she was so perky, too nice to be big. And Dermot Mulroney? The same way, a regular friendly guy. He laughed at my sheepherder jokes. (If they weren't sexist and degrading, I'd tell one now)." I can also talk some trash, like "River was a mess. I overheard Peter saying that he blew a whole thirty-thousand-dollar day of shooting. The Gothic chick with the nose ring scored some X for him, he misplaced his motivation." He was an intense person. Even when he wasn't in front of the camera, he had this pensive squint like his contacts were bothering him or he was working on an algebra problem in his head. He seemed bothered when spoken to or called upon to do a scene. Not an irritable bothered, more like, "You're pestering me, but I will be gracious to you because you are only doing your job." Samantha Mathis had similar star quality.

Needless to say, I could truly identify with *Thing's* premise: Song-writers come to Country Music Mecca following their dream. Some find it, some fall in love, and the viewer gets an inside look at the Bluebird Cafe scene. However, if I'd been the producer, I would have treated the viewer to an In the Round and Tony Arata singing "The Dance," after dedicating it to his mother. It's an experience that always leaves me spellbound, misty-eyed, and knowing why I'm still here.

There were a couple of weird things about the movie. First of all, they had the extras check in at the wardrobe trailer, where they gave us all TV-cliché clothing, like sequined Porter Wagoner jackets and Dolly Parton boobs are the norm here. I got a Hoss Cartwright ten-gallon Stetson with a feather band that looked like an Indian headdress. I felt silly hanging out in the extra tent all night looking ready to go trick-or-treat-ing because y'all out there in Movieland

At the real Bluebird our set lights are a little less conspicuous.

still need to have us looking like the cast of *Hee Haw*. I can see you every day touring Nashville, trying to blend in on lower Broadway wearing Wrangler jeans, big belt buckles, boots, Garth and Reba T-shirts.

And then there were the accents that the actors conjured up when playing a local. Nashvillians don't talk like that. Of course, you can't know that unless you live here, like I do. And then, it was harder for them (sigh). They weren't doing a "real."

■   ■   ■   ■   ■

Pat Barber came to Nashville from Colorado to pursue his songwriting. The laconic wit in his songs definitely sets him apart in Music City. In addition to songwriting and appearing in The Thing Called Love, *he's opened up a halfway house for men in recovery and is pursuing his interests in the ever-growing world of the Internet.*

Bret Graham

I had been hanging around the Bluebird for a few months trying to make ends meet. Amy Kurland called one day to say Paramount Pictures was filming a movie, *The Thing Called Love*, and maybe I could pick up a few bucks as an extra.

After a call to the appropriate people, I was told to show up at the Hall of Fame Hotel at six o'clock the next morning. All the extras were told to go to the bus station. Peter Bogdanovich lined up ten cowboy types, and as he came to each of us, we said, "Howdy, how you doing?" He liked my Howdy and gave me the part. I had the opening line in the movie. Samantha Mathis gets off the bus. I'm sitting in the station and say, "Howdy, how you doing?"

So thanks to Amy and the Bluebird I got to spend the day with Samantha Mathis and Sandra Bullock.

■　■　■　■　■

Bret Graham is one of Amy's all-time favorite performers. A native of Oklahoma, Bret has performed in a one-man show about the life of Woody Guthrie as well as appearing in The Thing Called Love.

Richard Leigh

Richard Leigh with former waitress Jan Dowling.

My most memorable experience regarding the Bluebird has to be the time I was standing in front of the Bluebird while I was standing in L.A. Sounds crazy, doesn't it? The reason being, I was attending the 1993 Grammy Awards and the nominees party happened to be located on the set of the movie *The Thing Called Love*, about a girl trying to make it big in Nashville as a songwriter. There on the other side of the buffet table was a one-block replica of our little Nashville street. The Bluebird Cafe sat there right in the middle. It gave me a very comforting feeling, and Layng Martine and I, who were there together as nominees for our song "The Greatest Man I Never Knew," felt right at home. Our friends John Jarvis and Vince Gill were the big winners that night in our category, with their song, "I Still Believe in You." But I did come away with something: Every time I stand in front of the Bluebird on Hillsboro Road now, I get a free "trip" to L.A.

■   ■   ■   ■   ■

Richard Leigh came to Nashville from Richmond, Virginia, in 1974. Within two years of his arrival he had his first number-one song with Crystal Gayle's recording of "I'll Get Over You." That was followed by the pop and country smash "Don't It Make My Brown Eyes Blue." Plenty more hits followed, including "Somewhere in My Broken Heart" and "The Greatest Man I Never Knew." Leigh was inducted into the Nashville Songwriters Hall of Fame in 1994.

CHAPTER

8

THE COMPANY WE KEEP

STARS FALL ON THE BLUEBIRD

David Billings

My favorite memory speaks clearly of the fact that I was one of Amy's employees who had no aspirations of being part of the music business. It was a Writers Night, with John Prine as the headliner. I was barbacking, which meant that throughout the night I was moving beer and glasses up to the bar. Mr. Prine was standing at the end of the hallway with his guitar talking with several hopeful songwriters. I nicely asked him to try and keep the narrow hallway clear since it was, and probably still is, just wide enough to move a rack of glasses through without scraping one's knuckles. As the night wore on—some of those Writers Nights could challenge a person's patience—my battle with John grew more aggravated. Finally I let loose, insulting the man, his guitar, and anything else I could think of as I tried to carry three cases of beer by his entourage. Jennifer, the bartender, was shocked and tried to instill upon me the importance of who I had just insulted. I justified my action with some comment that I would not vacuum the stage if he was on it, so he needed to stay out of my way. Luckily this battle subsided with John taking the stage, but the interaction wasn't

Here's folk troubadour Ramblin' Jack Elliot with his pal and peer John Prine.

over just yet. After his performance and several conversations with people trying to pitch songs, the place emptied out to just three people. John sitting at the bar, Jennifer chatting with him while counting her bank from the night, and myself restocking the depleted beer cooler. He looked at me and said, "I like you," to which I answered, "So what." He went on with "Really, I just look at you as someone who is here just to work, not to try and be close to famous musicians." I was still the flippant adolescent and answered his compliment with some harshness that I cannot recall. In the time to follow, he and I always joked about this encounter whenever he played at the Bluebird, and he would give me an overdramatized wide clearance in the hallway. So to John Prine, I say, Thanks. If you had wanted to, you could have put me in more than half an inch of water, and I would have never made another Happy Enchilada at the Bluebird Cafe.

Joy Lynn White

Alas! I do remember a very exciting night about six years ago. It all started earlier that day at Amy Grant's farm. I was one of the lucky recording artists asked to sing on the *Maverick* movie soundtrack. Everyone met there to record the song "Amazing Grace." They also shot a video of the song too.

Well, standing mostly by himself was the gorgeous Mel Gibson, in the greenroom. So I thought to myself, "Hey, you only live once." I got my courage up, and introduced myself to him. He was very friendly and real, like a regular guy. We talked for a little while again

JOHN PRINE

John Prine has been an American folk/rock icon for nearly thirty years. Born in Maywood, Illinois, he grew up in a blue-collar suburb of Chicago. Prine first learned to play the guitar from his father, a steelworker and union president. He began to write his first songs while working as a postman in Chicago.

Prine began to play the folk clubs in the Windy City and became friends with songwriter Steve Goodman, best known for "The City of New Orleans" and "You Never Even Called Me by My Name." Goodman introduced him to Kris Kristofferson, who helped him land a deal with Atlantic Records, writing the liner notes for his first album. Kristofferson helped his career even further when he brought Prine onstage at the Bitter End, a Greenwich Village mainstay. Bob Dylan was in the audience that night and jumped up onstage to back him on harmonica.

Prine's first few albums established him as a left-of-center folkie with a penchant for dry wit and touching insight. "Sam Stone," "Hello in There," "Paradise," and "Angel from Montgomery" are some of his most memorable songs. He's been covered by artists such as the Everly Brothers, Johnny Cash, Lynn Anderson, John Anderson, Bette Midler, and Bonnie Raitt.

Prine has been a resident of Nashville for many years and a friend to the Bluebird since our earliest days. As humble as he is talented, he never likes to play a local gig where his name has been advertised, but he has shown up countless times to lend himself to various shows and benefits.

Since he lives just around the corner from the

when we were lining up to record the song. I found myself standing right beside him. Oh, man! And we picked back up talking and hanging. So I says to Mel, "Have you spent much time in Nash?" He replied, "Not really. I flew in once before but flew right out." So I says, "Well, I could sure show you a good time if you ever had the time." And he says, "Well, okay." I could not believe it! He changed his plans and stayed over for the night.

So, I met him and his people at the Pub of Love. This is all true, you can ask Radney Foster, 'cause he was there too. Anyway, then we went to the Station Inn. He'd never heard real bluegrass music. It was so neat! We sat across from each other. He's so good-looking and funny and smart. He would be perfect for me, but he's married. (Sigh.)

So we headed for the Bluebird. By then I had a buzz on and I can't remember who was playing, some folks In the Round. Who could remember anything that night but MEL?! We sat at a table by the windows. I mentioned to him that the first movie I saw him in was *Tim*. He was very impressed. He said no one ever knows of that movie. It was the first movie he made, and he was twenty-four. He also told me later that he was in the process of beginning to shoot *Braveheart*. So the night goes on and he keeps wanting me to get up and sing, but I didn't want to ask. It's not my style. So it was getting late, bars were closing down, and we head to his hotel. When we get there we say our good-byes and nice to meet ya's, and he kisses me goodnight. YES, LADIES. MEL GIBSON kissed me! What a night to remember. Me and Mel Gibson. If I had to do it over again, I would've got up onstage and sang a song for Mel. Maybe next time.

■　■　■　■　■

Joy Lynn White has a voice that stops people in their tracks. After two albums on Columbia, she released The Lucky Few *on Little Dog Records. It was named Album of the Year by several publications, including the* Washington Post, USA Today, *the* Nashville Scene, *and* The Tennessean.

Jennifer Kimball

So far as memorable nights at the Bluebird go, they'd have to be

1. Those very first In the Rounds with Thom Schuyler, Fred Knobloch, and Don Schlitz, and others.
2. A Steve Earle performance   I can't even remember who else was there, but Steve was fabulous, and made fun of the round being " 'et up with ballads," which they so often are!
3. The night Randy VanWarmer, J. D. Martin, Tom Kimmel, and I were playing and LAUREN BACALL and PETER JENNINGS came in!

Steve Earle, the rock/country demigod of Nashville, is always welcome in our little club.

■　■　■　■　■　■

Jennifer Kimball has a knack for writing songs with enormous crossover potential. "Bop" and "I Can Love You Like That" made both the pop and country charts She's also been covered by Linda Ronstadt, Linda Davis, and Maura O'Connell.

117

CHILI SHACK

Since the Bluebird first opened its doors, we've done everything from poetry readings to jazz fusion, comedy to rock and roll, world music to country. One show that incorprated at least two of those elements— comedy and country—was the Chili Shack. So named for the free chili available at every show, Chili Shack was the brainchild of guitarist Brent Moyer and emcee Austin Church. While it made its debut at the now defunct Bogies Club in 1987, the Shack soon found its permanent address at the Bluebird.

The Chili Shack was a musical-comedy revue with special guests each month. The band included Billy Livsey on keys, Richard "Sticks" Stickley on drums, and Jon Vogt on the bass. Providing the comic relief was Daniel "T-Bone" Sarenana as well as Austin. T-Bone's two most famous characters were Juan Juan, a slightly shady Latin lawyer/lover, and Whitey Buck, "Country Music's Happiest Performer."

Over the years the special guests on the Shack were drawn from the entire spectrum of Nashville's talent as well as performers from abroad. Faith Hill, Chris LeDoux, Don Schlitz, Gary Burr, Joe Diffie, and Steve Forbert are just a few of the notables. We'll let Brent tell the story of a couple more very special guests.

Brent Moyer

I remember when Donna Summer was going to be our guest on Chili Shack. *Entertainment Tonight* would be filming it. We're all sitting around the Bluebird in the afternoon waiting for Donna to show up so we could rehearse the program. Everyone was a little bit nervous. Me too, because I usually got a tape of the songs the artists were going to do before the rehearsal so I could make charts and give tapes to the guys in the band so we would be prepared for the rehearsal as well as the show. Well, I had no idea what was going on because I never got a tape. To top it off, the television crew from *Entertainment Tonight* was running around doing their thing, setting up their lights, which just made the atmosphere in there a little more hectic than usual. So up pulls a big white stretch limo, and out pours Donna and her entourage. She comes waltzing through the front door, kinda stops, looks around for a second, and says, "Well, I guess you know who I am. Who are you?" That put everybody at ease right off the bat. We made our introductions, and I proceeded to tell her how the show was going to go. Then we got up and tried to figure out what we were going to do, write some charts, et cetera.

Her husband was going to play some songs he'd just written, and he couldn't play them the same way twice, so we didn't know how it was going to go on the show that night. Anyway, we worked up Donna's songs and went home, then came back to a packed house and bright television lights. The show went on. We got to their segment, and the band was great—we got through Donna's husband's songs without a hitch. When we got to Donna's portion of the show, she brought down the house with a robust version of "She Works Hard for the Chili."

Probably the most heartfelt and powerful performance I ever experienced at the Bluebird was when Alex Harvey was our special guest. He is such a soulful man. I just love him. He was up on the stage doing his set and the band was kicking as good as we ever had and the audience was being blown away and giving it right back to us. T. Graham Brown was in the audience, and Alex called him up to do "Hell and High Water," which they had written together. Let me tell ya, when he got done up there and the two of them got into that song, the magic really

SHAMELESS NAME DROPPING

We know it's a little shallow, but we just can't help ourselves. When the stars drop in, we have to drop their names from time to time. Here are a few we've had the pleasure of serving a brew to—or something like that.

CHET ATKINS
PETER CETERA
JON BON JOVI
BONO
MARK KNOPFLER
GEORGE BENSON
NEIL DIAMOND
LAUREN BACALL
MEL GIBSON
PETER JENNINGS
TOMMY SHAW
KEVIN BACON
GEORGE STEPHANOUPOLOS
GOVERNOR DON SUNDQUIST
VICTORIA JACKSON
RICHARD MARX
JOHNNY CASH
GEORGE JONES
PAUL BRADY
MARY BLACK
JUICE NEWTON
ASHLEY JUDD
LEVON HELM
JOHN KAY

(continued)

happened. When we finished the song, the whole room stood up and went crazy. I had never seen a standing ovation like that from the Bluebird—ever. Everyone in the place was on their feet, screaming and yelling. Then T., with tears in his eyes, I believe, proceeded to say how it was a special moment for him because he had not performed at the Bluebird since he landed his record deal from a performance there a few years before. He especially thanked Amy and Austin. I was just real proud to be a part of the magnificent moment.

There were many great moments with some of Nashville's finest songwriters, like Don Schlitz, Gary Burr, Rich Fagan, and Kostas, to name a few. We always liked to think of the Chili Shack as the stepping stone to stardom because many artists who performed on the show were discovered and had record deals soon afterward: Joe Diffie, Cledus T. Judd (no relation to the Judds), Chris LeDoux, Ethel and the Shameless Hussies, and Allison Moorer. And hats off to the Chili Shack crew: Austin Church, my cocreator and partner, T-Bone, a.k.a. Dan Sarenana, the band, Didi, and all the folks who kept coming back for more. And special thanks to Amy for believing in us.

Favorite Chili Shack recipe: Suede Bucket's Montana Red's Surefire Chili Pleaser. When asked about his recipe, he said, "Oh, my wife, Eloise, makes it; I just slap my name on it."

SHAMELESS NAME DROPPING

MICHAEL NESMITH
DAN FOGELBERG
MINDY MCCREADY
STEVE CROPPER
THE HOOTERS
PETER YARROW
DONNA SUMMER
HAL DAVID
J. D. SOUTHER
TRAVIS TRITT
JOHN SEBASTIAN
DOBIE GRAY
ALABAMA
SENATOR FRED THOMPSON
DAWN RUSSELL
LUKA BLOOM
STEPHEN BISHOP
CRYSTAL GAYLE
SHAWN COLVIN
TODD RUNDGREN
BRIAN WHITE
KINKY FRIEDMAN
JANE WIEDLIN
CHARLOTTE CAFFEY
ARLO GUTHRIE
LEO KOTTKE
THE INDIGO GIRLS
JOHN HIATT
JIMMY HALL

· · · · ·

Brent Moyer is, among other things, musical director for the long-running Chili Shack show. When not involved in that, he tours America and Europe sharing his own brand of country and folk. Raised in the mountains of Wyoming, Moyer is also lead guitarist for Lynn Anderson.

The Chili Shack finally went the way of the dinosaur, but we have many fond memories of their wild and crazy nights. We miss the band and the cast of characters the show brought to the 'Bird each month. And we really miss the chili.

CHAPTER 8 1/2

WHERE WOULD HE BE WITHOUT US?

GARTH AND THE BLUEBIRD

Somewhere in the dark recesses of Amy's office you'll find hanging on the wall the autographed audition sheet of a fellow by the name of Garth Brooks. The date is June 6, 1987. He'd been in town only a month. He got an A on his audition and was scheduled to play his first Writers Night a month later. Rumor has it Amy was so taken by him she walked up onstage and asked him to marry her. Alas, he was already betrothed.

Years later, when Amy dug up the audition sheet and had him sign it, Mr. Brooks wrote, "Amy, you'll never know how much you helped me. I love you. Love. God bless. Garth Brooks." So no ring, just his undying appreciation. And he owes us. Cool.

The tale has been told many times of how the Bluebird helped Garth solidify his deal. Here are a few more tales from those who watched it happen.

The high marks Garth Brooks received on his audition sheet for Writers Night was just a foreshadowing of his success. He's now the highest-selling solo artist ever.

Curtis Wright

The exact year escapes me, probably 1987 or '88, when I was asked to do the ASCAP writers' showcase at the Bluebird. When my name was announced, I did my three songs, then tore down my guitar rig to make way for another performer who was also new to town. I had never met Mr. Brooks, only heard of him. He shook my hand, and I said, "Son, I can't wait to hear you." He said, "Well, I've got my work cut out for me, having to follow you!" Little did I know that in a matter of months, we would all be following Garth Brooks!

•   •   •   •   •

As a writer Curtis Wright hits the mark every time. This laid-back hit maker's list of songs includes "A Woman in Love," "Next to You Next to Me," "Too Much Fun," and "Takin' the Country Back."

Ralph Murphy

Several years ago I was scheduled to play a showcase at the Bluebird. I was one of the "old dog" songwriters they were using as bait to get an audience so they could showcase some of the talented "new pup" writer/artists in town. A friend of mine in A & R at Capitol Records, Lynn Shults, was coming out to hang with me and then go have a beer after the show. Twenty-four hours before the gig, the label I was producing an act for called and wanted a remix done on the West Coast on the single they planned to release, and of course they wanted it yesterday. I left a message with the showcase organizers that apparently never got through, saying I would be out of town on the day of the show. Lynn told me when I got back to town that night that the organizers were freaking out trying to find me until one of the new pups volunteered to take my place. Lynn said for him it worked out great because even though he had turned down that singer-songwriter the week before he was so impressed by the performances that night that he signed the artist the very next day.

For me that was wonderful news because although I didn't know that artist that well back then, everyone working with him was almost like family (producer, management, et cetera). I was knocked out. Other than Lynn calling me No Show Murphy and buying me a beer when the artist had a number-one, time went on and I never mentioned the story to anyone. The showcase and the circumstances became just an amusing, seldom repeated story of the serendipity of the music business, until I got a call from my mother ripping me new body parts. She had been watching TV, and the artist told the story on national television that he got his record deal because Ralph Murphy did not turn up for the show at the Bluebird. To my mother "Thou shalt not miss a gig" is the eleventh commandment, and breaking it seemed to bring into question not only her abilities as a mother but the distinct possibility that I'd been switched at birth. I just visited my eighty-five-year-old mother, and I'm here to tell you that it's still a *hot* topic.

From Garth Brooks I heard "Thanks for not turning up at the Bluebird, pal." What I heard from my mother is unprintable.

■　■　■　■　■

Spend a few moments with Ralph Murphy, and his love for songs and songwriters will be crystal clear. His songwriting highlights include "Don't Take Me Half the Way" and "Seeds." These days he's helping new writers as the head of Writer Relations for ASCAP.

John Briggs

It's great how Garth Brooks today is the same friendly, unassuming guy he was in the early days when he was attempting to break into the business. Initially, Garth would hang out in the ASCAP lobby, or in Bob Doyle's ASCAP office. Bob later became Garth's manager. Garth was extremely inquisitive, often asking music business questions at the drop of a hat. One day Bob pulled me aside to listen to a tape of Garth's, which showed a remarkable songcrafting ability, but when Bob started pitching him to labels, they all passed on signing him. Bob did not give up.

At that time, I was serving on the Nashville Entertainment Association board, and a new concept was being developed by a fellow board member Pricilla Riggs. The idea was to create a series of showcases at the Bluebird Cafe for smaller publishers to display their songs for producers and record company A & R personnel. By this time Bob had left ASCAP and had mortgaged his home on his belief in Garth.

One day, during a luncheon with Bob, he played a few newly written songs of Garth's. One song in particular stood out. It was "Too Young to Feel This Damn Old." I told Bob, "That's a hit!" Later I talked to him about submitting a tape of the song to the first NEA Publishers Showcase at the Bluebird Cafe. Bob submitted his tape after the submission deadline, but, with a little bit of nudging, the commitee made allowances for his late submission. Once accepted, all the publishers and writer-performers were required to join the NEA. Since I had solicited Bob, I was given the task of informing him of his selection as a participant, and collecting the expected fees of $35.00 from him and $35.00 from Garth. Bob didn't like the idea of paying $70.00 for the right to perform at the showcase even though the money went to the NEA, a nonprofit organization to fund similar events, but after a couple of calls, Bob agreed to pay the fees.

A number of publishers submitted tapes for the showcase but we could only acept five. Each publisher's submission was given a numerical grade based on content. Thus, the higher the number the better your overall score. After the review process was completed, the committee took the top five scores. The highest score obtained was from David n'Will Music. It included the song "Sacred Ground," which would go on to be a number-one song for McBride and the Ride. Second in votes was Major Bob Music with "Too Young Too Feel This Damn Old." Garth was positioned next to last, to perform his future hit. Confident and poised, Garth electrified the audience the night of the showcase. In the audience was Lynn Shults, A & R for Capitol Records, who had initially passed on signing Garth. The performance Garth gave that night changed Shults's mind, and Garth was soon signed to the record label. The rest is history!

▪ ▪ ▪ ▪ ▪

John Briggs was born in Killen, Alabama. His highly successful career with ASCAP began in 1985. Currently he is the vice president of Membership Group. Over the years he has been responsible for bringing artists such as the Dixie Chicks, Alan Jackson, the Cranberries, and the Backstreet Boys into the ASCAP family. He is also a member of the Country Music Association, the Gospel Music Association, and the Nashville Songwriters Association International.

Becky Hobbs

In 1989 my band and I were constantly on the road promoting my *All Keyed Up* album, which had come out the year before. It was a Tuesday night in October, and we had just rolled up from God knows where. I was scheduled to play Okie Night at the Bluebird with Bill Caswell, Kevin Welch, Verlon Thompson, and others. Well, a cat I'd never heard of named Joe Diffie sang. And boy, did he SING! Blew me away.

And then a guy who was just starting to make some noise got up and sang a song that he had just cowritten, "Unanswered Prayers." Yep, it was Garth Brooks, and you could hear a pin drop. What a great song! He was mesmerizing, and the room was filled with a presence that was far more than the man, far more than the moment. That's when I knew he'd be a superstar. I'm proud of all the humanitarian things he does. This is my favorite Bluebird Cafe memory.

At an Oklahoma Writers Night, the world's most famous Okie, otherwise known as Garth, shares a few tunes while Buddy Mondlock chimes in.

■　■　■　■　■

Becky Hobbs first hit the airwaves with a duet with Moe Bandy, "Let's Get Over Them Together." Her album All Keyed Up *established her as a new and exciting star. She's performed in thirty-five nations and penned hits for many artists, including Alabama's "Angels Among Us."*

Jeff Pearson

I've been hosting the Sunday Writers Night at the Bluebird for ten years. One Sunday night, while walking back to where I sit after introducing the next songwriter, I looked to the doorway—wide open. Standing there in sweatpants and a windbreaker, with no hat of any kind, is Garth Brooks.

I walked up to him and said, "You're the bravest man alive to just stand there in the doorway." He said, "Are there any seats?" I said, "Follow me." As we walked through the crowd, people's faces went from casual indifference to awestruck disbelief as they recognized Garth. Nobody bothered him until we took a break. That's when it began.

Garth was converged on by about thirty-five to forty autograph seekers. He graciously signed his name for every single one, smiling, talking, and just being the down-to-earth guy he is. On the very last autograph, the woman had presented him a with a cocktail napkin and had turned her back to talk to someone else. Garth signed it, waited for her conversation to lull, tapped her gently on the shoulder, and offered her the autograph. She took it and went right back to her conversation.

Sunday Writers Night host Jeff Person could be talking about bass fishing, the Piggly Wiggly, or Demetria Kaledemos.

I marveled at Garth's poise and manners. He was the perfect gentleman. He had told me he just wanted to come to the Bluebird, hear a few writers, and relax. Sandy, his wife, was at home, pregnant with their first child. I told Garth, "Man, you handled all them people great!" He just said, "Thanks."

Then I got to thinking . . . He had three beers the whole time he sat next to me. He never once got up to go to the bathroom. He was probably thinking, "I don't need any autograph seekers in the men's room after me." He was probably right.

■ ■ ■ ■ ■

If you walk into the Bluebird and hear an emcee onstage talking about bass fishing, Piggly Wiggly stores, and Demetria Kalademos, you've found the host of our Sunday Writers Night showcase, Jeff Pearson. A California native, Pearson has had cuts in both the country and gospel fields.

Kent Blazy

I have many incredible memories of playing at the Bluebird's In the Round with some of my favorite writers. However, the Bluebird night that changed my life was one when I wasn't there.

Garth Brooks was playing with a bunch of new writers, but one of them, who was scheduled to play earlier, didn't show. Garth was asked to fill in his time slot. For some months prior to this fateful night, Garth and his manager, Bob Doyle, had sought a record deal and had been turned down by all the major labels. All of this was a little discouraging, but Garth and Bob were not ones to give in to these rejections. That night at the Bluebird, Lynn Shults from Capitol Records was listening when Garth played "If Tomorrow Never Comes," the first song we had written together. Lynn liked what he heard and asked Garth to come in to talk with him the next morning. The rest of the story has been told many times. Capitol offered Garth a record deal, and "If Tomorrow Never Comes" was the second single off his first album, titled *Garth Brooks*. It was the first number-one off the album and the first number-one for both Garth and me. *Thank you, Bluebird,* for establishing the environment for these little miracles to occur.

■　■　■　■　■

Kent Blazy and Garth Brooks have had a pretty good run together with songs like "Ain't Goin' Down 'Til the Sun Comes Up" and "If Tomorrow Never Comes."

Now we'll let Garth himself tell the story.

Garth Brooks

Like all things good, my story of the Bluebird Cafe does not speak of just one night but of several nights that shaped my career. The first time I ever met Amy I thought a friend of mine in the business had told her about me. The great thing about Amy is you never have to wonder where you stand with her. To call her direct would be an understatement, so twenty seconds into this conversation I could tell she didn't have a clue who I was. Looking back now, I realize she knew who I was more than I did. I was the face like a thousand faces before me, and the advice she gave me that night is the same advice I now give to anyone starting out in the music business. She simply said, "Slow down. The long run is what's important," which was just what I needed to hear.

My next brush with Amy and the Bluebird was at an audition for the infamous Bluebird Sunday Writers Night, which you had to audition for weeks in advance. I, like always, was late. Amy graciously waited and let me perform. Later I was notified that I was going to be able to play the Writers Night. I know this is going to sound strange coming from me, but the only thing I have ever wanted from this industry is to be accepted as part of the industry. The night I got to play the Bluebird for the first time, Amy introduced me like she did all the writers. It was after my first performance that she approached the microphone and, in her way, asked me to marry her. I laughed along with the rest of the crowd, but inside I felt a warm smile of acceptance. Only time would show how many more huge nights the Bluebird would give me and my music.

The Nashville Entertainment Association had a showcase at the Bluebird in which I was to perform. As a writer, to perform at the Bluebird is an honor, and at that point in my life I was also trying to be an artist. All seven major labels had just passed on me as a possible artist. I, of course, was devastated and did not want to go through with my commitment to play an NEA Publishers' Night. Bob Doyle, who has been my friend and manager forever, convinced me that my chance to play at the Bluebird was to be taken advantage of. I still didn't want to do it, but I knew he was right. I was about to find out just how right he was. I was scheduled to perform seventh out of nine writers. The writer who was supposed to go on second in the show was not there. The organizer of the show saw me sitting there and asked if I would be the second performer. Lynn Shults of Capitol Records was there to see the guy who never showed up. Lynn Shults saw Garth Brooks instead. When my performance was over, he was waiting offstage. What he said to Bob and me would change my life forever. He said, "Maybe we missed something here. Come to the label tomorrow. Let's talk."

Thinking that would be the biggest gift the Bluebird would give my career, I found myself corrected again. After getting my artist deal, I drifted from Writers Night to Writers Night, listening for songs. The Bluebird had already given me probably the most important night of my career. I was sitting in a room

The Birchmere in Alexandria, Virginia, hosts a Bluebird show featuring Russell Smith, Darden Smith, David Wilcox, Pat Alger, and Mark Germino.

with only a few others, when a songwriter by the name of Tony Arata took the stage. In his short set, a song called "The Dance" was played, yet another gift I was given. I could not picture my life without the song or the songwriter. The Bluebird gave me both.

Poised as a young artist whose career could gain speed with an accepted sophomore album, we had a song called "Friends in Low Places" out at the time. I was at the Bluebird one night with songwriter and friend Pat Alger. Big singles are a blessing to an artist. But they can also be a curse, if you cannot follow them up with another song of substance. At the Bluebird that night Pat and I decided at the last moment we would try a new song out on the crowd. The song was called "Unanswered Prayers." Immediately after the first chorus there came a round of applause, which I had never had before. It was a moment that made me feel like the song had reached inside everyone's soul who was listening. From that moment, we had no doubt "Unanswered Prayers" would follow "Friends in Low Places."

Throughout all the years, this industry has changed a million times, and in a world of changing waters, we all look for a rock to stand upon. In my opinion, the songwriter is the foundation of music and the Bluebird is the rock on which that foundation sits. The Bluebird has my gratitude, and Amy Kurland has my respect and my love.

■　■　■　■　■

Garth Brooks is the biggest-selling solo act in the history of the music industry.

CHAPTER 9

MAGIC AND MENTORS

Magic. When it comes to music and performing, you can't force it and you can't fake it. But when it happens, you know it, and it's something you never forget. We're happy to say that we've had more than our share of magical moments over the years. A special night, a special guest, a special song—they happen over and over at the Bluebird.

One of the most common "magic" moments around here is when a new writer hears a musical mentor. "Life-changing" is a phrase that is often heard.

Kenny Chesney

I played the Bluebird many times when I first moved to Nashville, and every time I played I got more confidence. But I was always intimidated by all of the great writers who performed there. Nowhere else in the world can you hear so many great songs. I have always been a big Michael Johnson fan, and I saw him perform one night when I first moved to town. I heard him sing "Bluer Than Blue," and I realized that night that I had a *lot* of work to do to become a great singer-songwriter. I'm still working toward that today. Hearing all the great singer-songwriters at the Bluebird really got the fire burning inside me and gave me a level to shoot for.

■ ■ ■ ■ ■

Hailing from Knoxville, Tennessee, Kenny Chesney began playing in Nashville at clubs like the Bluebird and the Turf before he caught the ears of executives at Acuff-Rose Publishing. Not long after that, he had a recording contract and hits like "You Had Me from Hello," "That's Why I'm Here," "She's Got It All," and "She Thinks My Tractor's Sexy."

keith urban

You know the story.

A drunken friend calls you late at night from some party and tries to get you to come over. For me it was usually a Monday-night "Hey, keith, you better get your Aussie butt down here right now 'cause the Bluebloods are tearing the roof off the joint!"

I would usually get in my car and go down into the mayhem, the music, the madness, and the magic that is the Bluebird. Of all the countless times I've been there, the one time that still makes me smile is the classic "first time."

It was September 1989, and my manager and I were visiting Nashville. We'd just spent the entire day taking my demo tape to all the labels and to unwind after all the rejection we went to visit the Bluebird Cafe. I sat and listened as Thom Schuyler, Craig Bickhardt, Fred Knobloch, and Don Schlitz took me from laughing to thinking to singing to even crying over a damn old house. Their songs, their stories, their camaraderie were all made that much more powerful by the ambiance of the Bluebird. She's the nest that's hatched many a gifted songwriter. If I sound like a fan, it's because I am. I've stood in line.

I've played the stage, In the Round, sat in the crowd, and been the last one to leave. It will always hold a very special place in my memory. God bless you, Amy.

■　　■　　■　　■　　■

keith urban left his native home of Australia for the Music Row and began impressing American audiences with incomparable guitar work and ample songwriting skills. His solo debut album yielded the hits "Your Everything," "It's a Love Thing," and the number-one smash "But for the Grace of God."

Jaime Kyle

When Amy called me and asked me to write a story about the Bluebird, I was on my cell phone, in Atlanta, in a dressing room. The first thing that came to my mind was a story about my father. Several years ago I was an upcoming rock artist/singer-songwriter. The best place to play in Nashville was the Bluebird. If you played the Bluebird, then you were SOMEBODY. So I finally got a chance to play. Am I somebody yet?

A week before I was to perform, I had written a song about leaving home, called "No Sad Good-byes." I was (I emphasize *was*) a headstrong, strong-willed personality. My father had a hard time controlling me. Actually, he couldn't, and I don't blame him for being bewildered. Hence "Wild One." Anyway, my father (Jim) and I were actually a lot alike. He would never tell you that, but looking back, I know it's true. I played him the song "No Sad Good-byes." I remember his face. He loved it. He played it over and over. He himself played harmonica and was very musical, and also a great storyteller. So for him to really like the song meant something. A couple of lines from the song were

> *When I die I hope no one cries, just let the music play,*
> *Above my grave the stone should say,*
> *"Let there be no tears today" and no sad good-byes,*
> *no sad good-byes.*

Life is so ironic. Songs sometimes foretell the future. Maybe it's your intuition that gets put down on paper, or what you couldn't verbalize to another human being. For me it was the Holy Spirit preparing me for my father's death. He came home from work (two days before my Bluebird show) and had a massive heart attack. Needless to say, my priorities in life got straight real quick. My life was forever changed.

I didn't cancel the show. I knew my father would want me to play. He encouraged me to live my dreams. But anyway, I showed up, tears and all. I tried to hide my grief, but when it came to doing "No Sad Good-byes," I lost it. Right in the middle of the song. I had to walk outside and collect myself. I missed my father intensely. I made it through the rest of the night and have since done many shows at the Bluebird, without crying.

About a year ago I was asked to be the featured writer on a Sunday Writers Night, and I said, "Great." Well, sometimes you feel things before your brain catches up. I do that a lot. It was Father's Day. I didn't realize it because I had felt left out on Father's Day. So every year I made a point not to notice. I was onstage and had this great idea. I said, "You know, I haven't done this song in a long time. I'm going to try to do it for you." Well, once again I broke down crying, in public. The audience reacted tenderly. They appreciated seeing that I had real feelings, and they were endeared. Myself, I was embarrassed and incredibly vulnerable in front of a lot of people. Eventually I got over it.

All that to say that the Bluebird is special to me. I have shed many tears there. Most of them were from laughing so hard I couldn't breathe. There aren't many people who care about the songwriters and their artistry. Amy Kurland does. She has given many songwriters as well as artists a place to be appreciated. What a gift to be able to perform your own songs for people who really want to hear them. Thank you, Amy, and everyone who works at the Bluebird.

■　■　■　■　■

In addition to penning the hits "Wild One" and "Stranded," Jaime Kyle has released two solo albums of her own, The Passionate Kind *and* Untangled.

Al Anderson

I think most of the writers who perform at the Bluebird play the room because it's an outlet for them to perform in an artist mode. Alas, if I never see a bus, hotel, dressing room, sound check, or venue again, it will be too soon. I love playing the Bluebird 'cause I'm always there with Bob DiPiero. It automatically becomes a party and a bunch of fun the whole night through. (I've already done twenty-three years on the road with NRBQ, and that's enough of that.) Sure, there're a few sad songs thrown in, but it only serves to make the night even more cool.

When I first came to town, I went to a few Writers Nights at the 'Bird, and as a patron it always bothered me to see four songwriters taking themselves so seriously. After all, it's just a song, and whether it made a million dollars or it's better than a Bob Dylan, it's always better to see people leave with a smile and feeling good.

And, of course, I always look forward to my letter from AFM 257 for having forgotten to file a contract to play there, 'cause I always forget. What the hell, I thought I was going to a party.

A special thanks to Amy for making the 'Bird a one-of-a-kind phenomenon. *Shhh!!* Also, remember to go see Mike Henderson and the Bluebloods on Monday nights. It should be a monthly requirement for people in the music biz to remind them what it's really all about.

• ▪ • ▪ •

Al Anderson left one of rock's most beloved bar bands, NRBQ, to pursue a career in songwriting. It was a good move. He has since had his songs recorded by artists such as Hal Ketchum, Aaron Tippin, the Mavericks, and Trisha Yearwood. His biggest hits include "Unbelievable," recorded by Diamond Rio and Carlene Carter's "Every Little Thing." He recently released his debut solo album, Pay as You Pump, *to unanimous rave reviews.*

Kenya Walker

I love the Bluebird Cafe and the standard it represents to the songwriting community. The Bluebird is a mecca of inspiration for songwriters starving for what they hope to be, what they have to be, and what they used to be.

My first Bluebird experience was when my longtime precious songwriter friend Steven Dale Jones took me there when he was scheduled to play the early show with Jim Martin, Bobby Tomberlin, and Tony Arata. It was 1989, I think, and it was cold outside. I didn't know what to expect other than four guys taking turns singing their own songs in a circle. I drove 120 miles to meet Steve in Athens, Alabama, at exit 351, and I rode with him the last 100 miles so happy to be with my friend who I rarely saw. We talked a streak, and he, being the good-hearted songwriter he was, shared stories unselfishly with me of his experiences in the music business. I was so hungry for any information about how you become a professional songwriter, I was in songwriter heaven in his company. We got to Nashville around 2 P.M., if I remember right, and Steve met with Jim and Bobby to practice in an old abandoned building. Jim and Bobby were great, and I've never laughed so hard.

That night at the show Steve made sure I had a good up-close seat so I wouldn't miss a note. After the first song I was mesmerized, carried away on the waves of passion living in their heartfelt songs, songs that said to me, "It's okay, Kenya Walker, for you to say whatever is lying at the depth of your heart that you are afraid for anyone to know." I longed to be invited into that intimate circle of serious songwriters. *Songwriter*—that is what I was too. I spoke, read, and wrote the language of the songwriter at that time, but it would be 1992 before I found myself with enough confidence and eight undeniable songs to swap and share.

When my Bluebird debut did come, I was so glad I'd waited till I had more than just okay songs to share. The people I was blessed to play with deserved more than good songs from me, and so did the audience. I would hate to look back on my first Bluebird performance and know that I would only be remembered for songs that were just okay but nothing special.

That first show I drove 225 miles to see led to my first performance at the Bluebird Cafe, and that led to my first taste of respect as a songwriter. That respect has led to staff writing deals, cuts on major artists' records, and a record produced by my hero in songs, Mr. Don Henry. More than those things, that first performance has led me to a higher quality of life than I could ever have imagined back in 1989—a life embraced by the most wonderful, precious people in the world, songwriters and lovers of great songs. So, Amy, my dear, thank you. I am so glad that my dream and yours matched a little bit. Thank you for the chair in the circle on numerous occasions, where I always find renewal and acceptance. I will try to always be worthy of that honored place at the Bluebird Cafe, at my Bluebird home.

■　■　■　■　■

Kenya Walker is our resident Southern diva. She's got style and attitude to spare. This native of Birmingham, Alabama, recently released her first album, Alligator Purse, *and had a hit with the Kippi Brannon single* "Daddy's Little Girl."

Angela Kaset

One night at a 'Bird In the Round, I played a brand-new song called "The Hopechest Song." Sony artist Stephanie Bentley was in the audience. She heard the song, and it moved her so deeply that she recorded it. I'll never forget hearing it debut on the radio on Christmas Eve. It was quite a shock, since we had given up hope of it becoming a single. It never became a big hit, but it charted, and lots of people all around the country heard it. To this day, people tell me this song was played at their wedding, or for the bride and her father to dance to, or just how it touched them in general. This is the only time I recall having a song recorded due to a live performance.

But just as important to me are the many times people have come to me after the show, occasionally with tears in their eyes, and named a particular song that was "their life." Quite often these are songs that are uncommercial, or at least unrecorded. Having an outlet for this material is very important to me as a writer. It keeps me fresh and hopeful.

■　　■　　■　　■　　■

Angela Kaset is a Tennessee native and one of our most dynamic artists. Her song "Something in Red" has become a signature tune for Lorrie Morgan. She's also had hits with "Daddy's Little Girl" and "The Hopechest Song." Her self-released album, Sanctuary, *showcases her distinctive style.*

Gail Davies

The only thing I can think of to say is probably that the first time I did a showcase at the Bluebird was for my record company. The band consisted of myself on guitar, Kevin Welch on acoustic rhythm, Gary Nicholson on electric lead, Wally Wilson on piano, Jack Sundrud on bass, and Martin Parker on drums. It was the dream band for sure, and everyone said I had the best-looking band in the business. That was back in 1982. Since then the

Two of our favorite Texans, Gary Nicholson and Lucinda Williams, pal around at the 'Bird.

Bluebird has been my home in Nashville and the place I've enjoyed playing the most in the twenty-five years I've lived here.

I love the Bluebird because it is a special place, a listening room where people come to hear and appreciate the music. That sets it apart from every other bar in Nashville.

■　■　■　■　■

Gail Davies forged the way for so many women in music today. As a songwriter, producer, arranger, and artist, she's set standards and precedents that have yet to be eclipsed. Her hits include "Round the Clock Lovin'," "Jagged Edge of a Broken Heart," and "Tell Me Why."

Jeffrey Steele

My history with the Bluebird Cafe started in 1988. I played my first showcase on that famous little stage with a new group from California called Boy Howdy. I remember showing up on a rainy afternoon as excited as a performer could be to play the club where so many had gotten their start. I was feeling the effects of a bad cold, though, and was worried about not being my best. My manager had heard someone say, "Get him some pickle juice. It's good for the voice!" I still think it was a cruel joke played on a rookie, but sure enough I had a jar of pickle juice five minutes later.

I was surprised at how small the club was. *Intimate* would be a better word, and my first thought was, "Geez. We shouldn't have brought all this gear! All we really need is acoustic guitars."

Well, the place was packed by six, and we started rockin'. We were so loud I think The Who would have been proud. I saw a lot of people making comments and pointing as I drank the awful-tasting pickle juice (must be from the West Coast) in hopes of enhancing my performance.

Needless to say, we didn't get signed that night, but on my next few trips to Nashville everyone would say, "Now, what's the deal with the pickle juice?" I thought, "Man, if we'd have gotten a deal, that pickle thing would have been quite a moneymaker."

But what made the biggest impression on me was seeing the pictures on the wall. I wanted to come back one day and play my hits. Well, it took a few years, but I finally got my chance, and to think I would get to play with songwriters like Kent Blazy, Craig Wiseman, Al Anderson, and Sharon Vaughn, to name a few. It's humbling and challenging at the same time. I have learned a lot about songwriting just by sitting there playing and hearing others sing—what to do, but more important, what not to do. I hope to one day have my picture on the walls of that small little place that is the proving ground of so many.

■　■　■　■　■

Jeffrey Steele was the lead singer and bass player for Boy Howdy. He wrote several of their hits, including: "A Cowboy's Born with a Broken Heart" and "She'd Give Anything." Steele was born and raised in and around Los Angeles. His songwriting credits also include cuts by Gerald Levert, Kevin Sharpe, and Diamond Rio. He is now an artist on Monument Records.

Harry Stinson

If you play the Bluebird as much as I have, something's gonna happen to you. The process of putting Kevin Welch's band together after I left Steve Earle in '88 happened at the 'Bird. We played there all the time. His two Warner Bros. records were woodshedded there. Mark Knopfler and Bonnie Raitt were among our visitors; Bonnie even jammed with us. We had a great time and kept things on the loose side, like the Saturday night there was a lunar eclipse, and Kevin interrupted our set to invite the whole club out to the parking lot to watch it. It was a very cool moment, and when it felt right, we wandered back in and finished the show.

The ice storm of '94 spawned another impromptu moment. The whole city was without power; I was for eight days. We were booked for a Saturday night and were wondering if the club would even be open. I don't remember how it shook down, but we decided to play acoustically. I brought in a small drum kit and even played a little acoustic guitar. From the first moment I walked into the club it felt really special. The place was packed, and I noticed the absence of the background music that normally plays, and, of course, light bulbs. The candles placed on every table furnished all the light. People were talking in hushed tones. When the time came, we just got up on stage and played. The entire room was completely transfixed. No need for the *Shhh* rule that night, you could feel everyone's concentration on the song, the performance. The sound of unamplified acoustic instruments and singing was absolutely magical. From where I was onstage it felt like a mini orchestra. We all found new, inspired ways to play songs we had been playing for years. We even later recorded some of the songs that way using no headphones. That night, though, was a night I will always remember, and as for the rumor of a woman who used too much hair spray and got too close to a candle, well, you'll have to ask Amy about that.

My worst nightmare: The fact that I said, "Sure, I'll come down and play a couple of songs," was my first mistake. Tree, my publisher at the time, was having a get-together for all their writers, staff, and the public at the Bluebird. I don't remember the year, but it was in the early nineties. Kix Brooks (pre Brooks & Dunn) was hosting, and the place was full of peers and famous songwriters. I was willing, but I was uncomfortable at the time simply because I had no experience accompanying myself. I was usually behind the drums during those years, and guitar playing was strictly limited to the writing session.

The numbness started when I left the house. I had a couple of songs picked out, and I started worrying that I wouldn't be able to remember the words. When I got to the club, it was a huge social event, but I had this tunnel vision thing going, trying to stay focused on my thing. I know I talked to people, but I must have seemed like a woman in labor. I was a walking robot.

I finally got the nudge to go to the side of the stage; my time was nigh. Kix had graciously offered the use of his acoustic, since I didn't have one that I could plug in, and as I sat down to wait my turn, my heart was clearly visible in my throat.

Just when I thought it was my time to be sacrificed, Walter Campbell whispered to me, "Hey, Roger Miller wants to play, but he's gotta split, so can he go in front of you?" I'm sure I said yes, but I don't remember. Roger took the stage and proceeded to take the place apart. He had people cheering, laughing, crying, and rolling in the aisles all at the same time. It was an amazing performance. Looking back, I was so fortunate to experience his gift at such close proximity, but at the time all I could think was I'm dead.

The place was all abuzz after Roger left the stage, on a real high. Then it was my turn. Kix introduced me and handed me his guitar. Nothing went right after that. The action on his guitar was unfamiliar, the sound was bizarre (to me), and after I managed to strap the thing on and get my capo set, I looked up and who's sitting and staring at me from the main table smack in front? Roger, Harlan Howard, Red Lane, and, I think, Curly Putnam (I've blocked some of this out). It felt like four Saint Peters waiting for me to show them why they should let me into heaven.

I must've started playing and singing. All I really remember is being in s-l-o-w motion, dreamlike motion. Except I wasn't gonna be able to wake up from this dream. Nobody was gonna save me, and, man, I needed saving.

Well, I survived. I do play guitar pulls and occasional Writers Nights from time to time, but it took me a good six years to get up the nerve!

■ ■ ■ ■ ■

As a background vocalist and studio drummer, Harry Stinson has probably been recorded more than anyone else in Nashville. In recent years he's put his talents to work as cofounder of the new, independent label Dead Reckoning. He also cowrote Martina McBride's big hit "Wild Angels."

Kacey Jones

I stepped into the Bluebird Cafe for the first time in 1986. It wasn't exactly the shrine I had imagined, but somehow I still felt like I was entering a church. That humble little room came alive for me that night, and I realized that not all shrines are created equal. Even then I recognized the importance of this little haven, in that more songwriting talent had graced its stage than any place I'd been.

Like every other songwriter I knew, I couldn't wait to get up on that stage. The concertlike atmosphere inspired me. I, for one, like the *Shhh!* cards that are displayed on each table as a reminder to grant the performer a little respect and appreciation. It makes me want to do my best when I perform there.

I've appeared at the Bluebird in many configurations over the years. First as a solo artist, and then with a band of gypsy songwriters that included Mickey James, Rich Fagan, Patty Ryan, Mark Irwin, Brent Moyer, and a couple of very talented gals, Valerie Hunt and Becki Fogle, who I later teamed up with to form the infamous Ethel and the Shameless Hussies. When the Hussies and I signed our deal with MCA Records, no one was more happy for us than Bluebird matriarch Amy Kurland. Amy gave us the chance to perfect our act on that stage. It was a wonderful time in our lives.

I left Nashville in 1990 but returned in 1994 after a four-year stint in L.A. The first place I went when I got back to the Music City was the Bluebird. It was like coming home to an old friend. I started performing there again with a raucous trio called "Phillybilly," which included the lovely and talented Rich Fagan and the equally lovely and talented Joe Collins. Phillybilly played a lot of places, but I always thought we were best when we played the Bluebird.

In 1997 I signed a solo deal with Curb Records and released a comedy album called *Men Are Some of My Favorite People*. Again, Amy gave me the chance to perfect my act on the Bluebird stage before hitting the road and the comedy-club circuit. It was valuable onstage time for me.

My most recent gig at the Bluebird was a double bill with Kinky Friedman. We had such a good time onstage that night that we're threatening to do it again. Look out, Amy!

I've encountered most of my favorite cowriters at the Bluebird. Whether I'm playing there solo, with a group, or In the Round, it is always an honor for me. It's a reverent little place, and I hope it lives on forever.

■ ■ ■ ■ ■

Kacey Jones scored her first hit with Mickey Gilley's cover of "I'm the One Mama Warned You About." In Nashville she's known as a member of Phillybilly with Rich Fagan and Joe Collins and as a solo artist and, more recently, a producer. Her hilarious live CD, Men Are Some of My Favorite People, *was released in 1997 on Curb Records.*

Les Kerr

In 1987 I moved to Nashville from the Gulf Coast and discovered the Monday-night Open Mic songwriters show at the Bluebird Cafe. It was hosted by Barbara Cloyd then, and performers at the "show-up, sign-up, and sing" event had enough time on most nights to do four songs. My goal was to be on as late as possible each night, so the audience for the headlining Kingsnakes blues band would catch my act as they were being seated. It worked and some Kingsnake followers became fans of mine. But the best part for me was to see people like singer-songwriter John Prine, actor David Keith (*An Officer and a Gentleman*), and songwriter Roger Cook ("I'd Like to Teach the World to Sing").

After I graduated to hosting weeknight early shows on my own, a thrilling moment came when Kathy Mattea arrived in time to see the last fifteen minutes of my show. She was there with her husband, songwriter Jon Vezner, to see that night's headliner, Don Henry. Henry and Vezner had written her hit "Where've You Been." Mattea was CMA Female Vocalist of the Year at the time, and after my show I introduced myself to her. She graciously complimented me on my songs and left me in a state of euphoria that lasted for weeks.

I'm very proud to have headlined the annual Mardi Gras shows at the Bluebird Cafe since 1992. The show has included everything from handing out doubloons to a small parade through the tables, making the audience a part of the production. Once a couple showed up in traditional Mardi Gras formal wear—white tie, tails, and ball gown and adorned with the holiday's staple accessory plastic beads.

Another encounter with John Prine occurred one Mardi Gras. Attempting to impress him after the show I told him that I had recently performed some of his songs in Kentucky. He was curious about which of his songs got the best response. I thought, John Prine is asking me how people like his songs. Wow!

I will never forget seeing Mary Chapin Carpenter open for Carlene Carter at the Bluebird. Grand Ole Opry star George Hamilton IV was in the audience. Such moments at the Bluebird Cafe make those of us who moved to Nashville to follow our dreams thankful we're here.

■　■　■　■　■

Les Kerr is a songwriter originally from the Mississippi Gulf Coast. With his Bayon Band, he has headlined Bluebird Cafe Mardi Gras shows since 1992. His CD Red Blues *was nominated for Blues CD of the Year by the Music City Blues Society in 2001. Kerr performs frequently in Nashville and throughout the United States.*

Mark T. Jordan

At the risk of sounding melodramatic, I can safely say that visiting the Bluebird for the first time literally changed my life.

In the spring of 1992 I was recently remarried and had made several trips to Nashville from my base in L.A., encouraged by my friends Kin and Carole Vassey (he was the second lead singer, behind Kenny Rogers, in the First Edition). On this trip Kin suggested we perk up a cold and drizzly Friday night in March by hopping down to the 'Bird and checking out the bill (like my ornithological references?).

There was a long line at the door (natch), and upon reaching the hostess's desk, we were told the show was sold out but we could claim James Stroud's table if he didn't show up. Well, he didn't and we did. The Writers In-the-Round that night? Only Billy LaBounty, Hal Ketchum, Gary Burr, and Hugh Prestwood. We sat about eighteen inches from Bill's right elbow. Wow.

As I heard such songs unfold as "Can't Be Really Gone," "I Wanna Be Loved Like That," and "Ghost in This House," I became equal parts awestruck and dumbfounded, not only by the depth of

Country superstar Mark Chesnutt was on hand to sing "I Don't Want to Miss a Thing" at songwriter Diane Warren's special night at the Bluebird.

this cumulative talent but by the audience's reverence and rapt attention. To a songwriter and pianist, it felt a lot like nirvana. I wanted this.

Long short story? Peggy and I bought a house in West Nashville in March '93 and moved in on June 10. In the ensuing six years I've had the great fortune to play with such "fabulons" (thank you, Robert K. Oermann) as Bonnie Raitt, Lyle Lovett, Delbert Mc-Clinton, and Wynonna, and have recorded with such legends as Hank Thompson and Patti Page. I have hosted a number of my own shows at the 'Bird. I've even written a song or two with ol' Gary Burr himself; one of 'em's called "The Sky's the Limit."

Wanna hear it?

■ ■ ■ ■ ■ ■

Mark T. Jordan has toured the world as a keyboardist for Van Morrison, Jackson Browne, Wynonna, and Bonnie Raitt. Since arriving in Nashville, he's developed the popular series of In the Rounds he calls "piano pulls."

Paul Jefferson

The Bluebird's reputation preceded my first trip to Nashville. I read about the stars who had been discovered there and the hit songs or soon-to-be-hit songs heard there every night. I had performed for years around my home in the San Francisco Bay Area, but I had never experienced such an intense vibe, an audience packed into a room that looked more like a gift shop than an internationally famous nightspot.

And they listened. They listened to every word. And I felt naked, with only a guitar to hide behind. It was terrifying and I loved it.

A few years later I got a chance to play with some of my songwriter heroes in the uniquely Nashville Writers in the Round. On one night I was playing with hit songwriter Monty Powell and the phenomenal artist-songwriter keith urban. Monty had thought up an entertaining gag for the evening, where we would pick from a hat a theme for each round of songs. Simple themes like heartache, comic, or artsy songs. One theme was number-one songs. Well, Monty was the only one among us who had a number-one song, "My Kind of Girl." After folks got the joke and laughed a little, keith and I played what we wished could be number-one songs. I played a song I cowrote with Jan Leyers and Sally Dworsky called "That's As Close As I'll Get to Loving You," which was rumored to have been just recored by Aaron Tippon. A few months later Aaron's version of the song was number one. Does the Bluebird have that kind of energy? I think so.

■　■　■　■　■

Hailing from California, Paul Jefferson came to Nashville intent on showing everyone he has what it takes to be a successful songwriter and artist. So far, so good. Aaron Tippin took Paul's tune "That's As Close As I'll Get to Loving You" straight to number one on the charts. Jefferson then hit the charts himself with "Check Please."

Victoria Shaw

The first time I ever went to the Bluebird was back in the mid-eighties, when I saw Paul Davis, Fred Knobloch, and Paul Overstreet. I sat there mesmerized by these incredibly talented men, just soaking up all that wonderful music. I really do believe that night was life-changing, because it both inspired and totally intimidated me! These were some of Nashville's premier songwriters, and I wanted to be part of that club so bad I could taste it. I've spent so

Artist Leroy Neiman spent a night at the Bluebird and sketched some lovely pictures of Gary Burr, Don Henry, and Marshall Chapman In the Round. The pictures are now hanging on the walls of the cafe.

many, many nights hanging out at the Bluebird since then, enjoying people like Marshall Chapman, Jill Sobule, Buddy Mondlock, Stevie

Winwood, Michael McDonald, Bonnie Raitt, and a hundred others that I don't have room to name. And you know what? Even though I now write songs for a living, I'm still totally inspired and intimidated by what goes on at the Bluebird Cafe night after night. I think that's what makes me work so hard to be the best I can be.

■　■　■　■　■

Who'd guess that a girl from New York would move to Nashville and write some of the most memorable classics in country music? That's exactly what Victoria Shaw has done. In addition to writing the Garth Brooks anthem "The River," she also had the honor of opening for Brooks when he played his concert in Central Park.

Cindy Bullens

I had heard so much about the mystical Bluebird Cafe before I ever stepped foot in Nashville that when I pulled into this tiny strip mall just outside the city, I was confused. I wondered what made this teeny little place so special. It didn't take long for my question to be answered. The level of songwriting talent under that roof absolutely

The subdudes were always one of our favorites. Their unique sound was a hybrid of pop, soul, and country.

stunned me. I became a Bluebird devotee each time I ventured back to Nashville, which was often, breathing in as much of that sweet creative air as I could. I was introduced to owner Amy Kurland through a friend, and one night Amy asked me if I wanted a slot to play three songs on a kind of "new talent" night. Now, I had had a pretty successful career ten years earlier in the rock and roll world, had played in front of thousands of people and had some recognition, blah, blah, blah. But to be asked to get on the Bluebird stage felt like someone had just asked me to perform at the Grammy Awards. And it scared the heck out of me. I hadn't stood alone with my acoustic guitar and sung a song for ten years. Let's just say that when I got up onstage that night, I might as well have been in Dodger Stadium. I sang my songs so loud and with so much energy that I'm sure those poor folks in the audience thought they had mistakenly walked in on a Rolling Stones concert. They applauded politely. A friend who was with me gently commented that maybe my voice was a little "too big for the room." Luckily, Amy asked me back again and we became friends, and as I became established in Nashville as a working song-writer, I continued to experience many wonderful nights there as a lis-tener and as a performer. And I am happy to say that I can actually sing a song onstage now without seeing the people sitting in front of me stuffing pieces of napkin in their ears.

■　　■　　■　　■　　■

A native of Newburyport, Massachusetts, Cindy Bullens is a Grammy-nominated rock and roller. She's performed with some of the biggest names in the business, including Elton John. Her credits also include three cuts on the Grease *soundtrack as well as cowriting the Radney Foster hit single, "Hammer and Nails."*

Ray Thornton

In the late eighties, Ashley Cleveland, Tricia Walker, Karen Staley, Pam Tillis (and others who took over Pam's spot) performed together as Women in the Round. I heard them first at the Bluebird Cafe and laughed my butt off through their "Nashville Rap." It was like sitting in my den with a bunch of friends, four of whom are really wonderful writers, singers, and musicians who really get a kick out of one an-other and playing for us all. Someone serves us drinks and food and we don't have to clean up afterward. But of course I have to pay for it and drive home, and my den is only about half the size of the Blue-bird.

Writers in the Round created an atmosphere where you thought you and the others in the room were having more fun than anybody else in town. Since then I have had the same blessing on dozens of nights with Walt Wilkins, Jen Cohen, Steve Conn, and so many oth-ers. And now sponCom gets to play there as well. We're well into our second year at the 'Bird and couldn't ask for a safer place to walk the edge. As I said, one of the wonderful qualities of the Bluebird is how comfortable a place it is for the audience, which is essential for im-prov.

When it's an In the Round show, you're right there with the artists. Even with the traditional stage setup, it is still incredibly intimate. Our most recent show there highlights its intimacy. I had just finished introducing our improv group, sponCom, and was warming up the audience to get them to throw out suggestions, when a woman at one of the center tables caught my attention and mouthed that my fly was down. Not only was it down, it was irreparably busted and had been for the entire introduction. I stepped back onto the stage, acknowledged my dilemma, thanked the woman for her warning, taped my fly closed, and the show picked right back up where it had left off. You don't get that at the Ryman.

■　■　■　■　■

Ray Thorton was one fourth of the hilarious improv group sponCom. He's also an actor and has recently relocated to Los Angeles, where he's beginning to land roles on several television shows.

Bob Regan

About ten years ago when I was stuck trying to get started I played an In the Round at the Bluebird. I played a song I had just finished writing with Mark Sanders (also just getting going) called "Here's Hopin." At the end of the night Kathy Mattea came up to me and said, "I want to cut this song." She held up her hand to show me where she had written the title on her palm. It was on *Willow in the Wind* and my first gold record.

■　■　■　■　■

Bob Regan came to Nashville from Sacramento, California. One of his earliest hits was Lee Greenwood's version of "We've Got It Made." That was followed by songs like "Soon," "Thinkin' About You," and "Runnin' Out of Reasons to Run."

Brett Jones

I came to Nashville in the summer of 1990 and started playing the Monday-night Open Mic religiously to become a member of the Nashville songwriter community. This experience helped me to get my first publishing deal, but more important, it gave me the inspiration to write my first number-one record, "You Gotta Love That" by Neal McCoy. The song is about one of my fellow struggling songwriters who I met at the open mike. Thanks to Barbara Cloyd and Amy for that opportunity.

■　■　■　■　■

"A Little Past Little Rock" and "Cover You in Kisses," two of Jones's better-known hits, both received awards from ASCAP for Most Played Songs in 1998. Neal McCoy, Tracy Lawrence, and Reba McEntire have also recorded his songs.

Jeff Black

I just always remember Amy being kind to me. You know, you hear things and don't know what to expect. But it was all good, from the first time I auditioned to play the Sunday-night show to having to use a crowbar to get Steve Earle after he got clean to come out of his cave to play. I met some of the best friends I've ever had, Mike and Bob Delevante, at the Bluebird. I always felt more like I was on a recon mission, an undercover agent in Nashville, and Amy embraced me first.

■　■　■　■　■

Jeff Black became a Bluebird favorite on the strength of his big, booming voice and his insightful songwriting skills. Edgier artists such as Shania Twain and BlackHawk have recorded Black's tunes. Arista Austin gave him his first record deal, and the result was Birmingham Road, *which featured members of Wilco as his studio band.*

Karen Taylor Good

My favorite Bluebird gig has to be my last. My hero, my friend, frequent cutter of my songs Collin Raye invited me and Tom Douglas to join him onstage for a charity gig. Ah . . . to be in an intimate setting like the Bluebird in that company, where every word of every song, every vocal nuance could be heard and felt—it was heaven. God bless the Bluebird! Long live the Bluebird! Hip hip hooray!

■　■　■　■　■

An artist looking for a ballad that will pull some heartstrings and climb the charts need look no further than Karen Taylor Good. Her "How Can I Help You Say Goodbye" was one of Patty Loveless's biggest hits and named by SESAC as one of the Most Performed Songs in 1998/1999.

Phil Vassar

My first round at the Bluebird will always be memorable to me. I'd never even had a single on the radio yet. I was playing with Skip Ewing, Don Sampson, and Tim Rushlow of Little Texas (all have had huge hits). It was for Tin Pan South, and it was a wonderful experience. I'd never met Don, and since then we've become good friends and we've written some cool songs. Playing with guys like this inspires you and takes your songwriting to another level. The Bluebird Cafe is THE PLACE where a songwriter can express himself and people can come to enjoy listening to the songs and the stories that brought the songs to life.

■　■　■　■　■

If overnight success takes ten years, Phil Vassar is right on time. It was about ten years ago that Vassar left his hometown of Lynchburg, Virginia, to pursue songwriting in Nashville. In 1998 he scored with "Postmarked Birmingham," "Little Red Rodeo," and "For a Little While." JoDee Messina had two number-one hits with Vassar's "Bye Bye" and "I'm Alright." He is now signed to Arista as a recording artist and has scored hits with "Carlene" and "Just Another Day in Paradise."

Richard Fagan

One evening a few years back I got a last-minute call to open for Gary Burr. Toward the end of my set, I did my John Michael Montgomery cut, "Be My Baby Tonight," which hadn't been released yet. When I got off the stage, I was surprised to see John Michael there in the audience (seated with Faith Hill, Scott Hendricks, and Victoria Shaw). He said, "When you hit the chorus, I started to sing along, but some lady tapped me on the shoulder and said, 'Shhh! You mind saving that for the break? This is a listening room!' "

■　■　■　■　■

Richard Fagan has given John Michael Montgomery three of his biggest hits: "Sold," "I Miss You a Little," and "Be My Baby Tonight." He's also had his songs recorded by Neil Diamond, Mel McDaniel, and Shenandoah.

Steve Seskin

The Bluebird has been an instrumental part of my Nashville career. Besides providing a supportive, quiet place to play, it's where I met Bob DiPiero. I was performing two songs on a Sunday in 1987, and Bob was the special guest. He liked my work and arranged an appointment with Woody Bomar at their company, Little Big Town Music. In a way, all the wonderful things that have happened in the last twelve years can be traced back to that one night. I also treasure my memories of all the In the Rounds I've done there. What a great concept! I love mixing it up with other songwriters. The Bluebird is, and will always be, at the top of my list.

■ ■ ■ ■ ■

Steve Seskin is another highly successful country songwriter who doesn't call Nashville his home. San Francisco is where he hangs his hat, but he makes several trips to Music City each year to write and pitch songs like "Wrong," "Life's a Dance," and "Use Mine."

Vince Melamed

Cookin' at the Bluebird. Heck, I thought this was going to be a cookbook. I was ready to submit my "blackened macaroni and cheese" recipe from college:

1. Pour Kraft macaroni and cheese along with some water in a pan.
2. Heat over huge flame.
3. Forget for an hour or two.

I do appreciate Amy's tolerance and sense of humor for permitting us to stage the debut and fizzle of Barney Mello Glo onstage in the mid- to late eighties, by the way. As far as romantic stories go, I admit I didn't actually meet Meredith (my wife) at the club. However, having her witness a Writers in the Round or two helped seal the deal. She saw I was the same knucklehead en masse as in private, maybe with a dash of romantic thrown in. And thanks to a showcase there in '90, I got my first big country cut when Greg Barnhill and I performed "Walkaway Joe" to Garth Fundis's delight at the Bluebird. 'Preciate it.

■ ■ ■ ■ ■

Vince Melamed has worked as a keyboard player with the likes of Bobby Womack. His writing credits include "What Mattered Most," "She'd Give Anything," and "Walkaway Joe."

JONELL MOSSER

As a performer, Jonell Mosser has gone through many incarnations. Whether she's singing with her first band, Yo Mama, Enough Rope, Kentucky Thunder (with Vickie Caricco, Sheila Lawrence, and Nannette Britt), or Girls Girls Girls (with Karen Staley and Lee Satterfield), she does it with all her heart. Born and raised in Louisville, Kentucky, Jonell has been singing from an early age. She came to Nashville in the latter half of the eighties to pursue her musical aspirations. It wasn't long before she was making her first forays into the clubs around town. She began to show up at the gigs of the Kingsnakes and sit in, singing one of her earliest signature songs, "You Don't Miss Your Water." She often did the same at the tiny club on Elliston Place (now defunct) known as Elliston Square, joining the Fever Blisters onstage.

As her vocal prowess became more and more obvious, she began playing steady gigs at the Bluebird with her band Enough Rope. In the early days the band included bassist Victor Wooten, now with Bela Fleck and the Flecktones, guitarist Tom Britt, who tours now with Patty Loveless, and Jimmy Greasy, who also played with Blue Monday.

A lot of Bluebird regulars have fond memories of her series of Monday-night and weekend shows, where she would play three sets, never letting up until the wee hours of the morning. The band was hot, the room was even hotter (we were in desperate need of a new air conditioner), and Jonell was fast becoming our biggest draw. In fact, Amy would eventually put it like this: "She is the record-holder on all scores—most bar sales, most door sales, and best female friend a music-club owner could have."

Of course talent this big can't be kept in our little room. Jonell's career has blossomed into many

Jim Collins

My favorite Bluebird memory is probably the night I saw Jonell Mosser. I had just moved from Texas and had never been around someone with that much soul. I'm not sure if it was the vodka or the excitement of her music. All I know is I somehow wound up onstage hugging her uncontrollably. She was AWESOME!

There are too many great moments to name them all, but I can honestly say the Bluebird has had a real impact on me and my desire to be a songwriter, and I hope they stay there forever. Thanks for letting me be a part of this scrapbook.

■　■　■　■

Jim Collins first made a name for himself as the reigning king of the dance-hall circuit in his native Texas. Since then he's become a hit songwriter, penning chart toppers like "Hands of a Working Man," "Yes," and "She Thinks My Tractor's Sexy."

Jess Leary

Back in the fall of 1990 I ventured out with a friend to catch a Bluebird show. To this day, I can't remember who was performing that evening. All I know is that I opened the door, paid the cover charge, and there she was. Not five feet away. Sitting at a table near the door, casually glancing back at me, was my idol, my hero, the most wonderfully gifted singer/song-writer/musician on the planet. For that moment, time stood still. I flashed back to memories of a teenage girl with my first guitar, wearing out the needle on my stereo. I knew every skip on her records, every word, every sound. When I was seventeen, "At Seventeen" was on the radio. I played "And in the Winter" so loud my older sister threatened to kill me. There she was, Janis Ian, not five feet away. I thought at that moment I was about to become the biggest dork she'd ever meet. If I could just walk right past her table and ignore the fact that there sat my greatest inspiration, the very reason for my pursuing a career in music.

That night changed my life. Turns out Janis didn't think I was a dork (or at least didn't say so), and through the years that followed we've become great friends and have written many wonderful songs together. All because of that fateful night at the Bluebird.

■   ■   ■   ■   ■

Jess Leary hails from the Boston and Cape Cod areas of Massachusetts. She spent years on the road as a back-up vocalist and guitarist with artists like Reba McEntire, Garth Brooks, Faith Hill, and Lari White. Her songwriting credits include two number-one smash singles "Mi Vida Loca" and "Where the Green Grass Grows."

JONELL MOSSER

facets. She quickly became sought after as a session vocalist and over the years has performed on albums by artists such as Etta James, Wynonna, Rodney Crowell, Bruce Cockburn, Jesse Winchester, Vince Gill, George Jones, B.B. King, Hank Williams Jr., and so many more. She's appeared onstage with the Fairfield Four, John Prine, Townes Van Zandt, Bonnie Raitt, Keb' Mo', John Gorka, Lyle Lovett, and Levon Helm.

For too many years fans and patrons would call the Bluebird office wanting to know where they could buy an album by Jonell and the answer was "Nowhere." That finally changed when Jonell released *Around Townes,* a collection of songs by Townes Van Zandt. That was followed by *So Like Joy,* an album of Jonell's unmistakable originals, many of them cowritten with John Hall of Orleans and his wife, Johanna. She's also released *First Christmas* and has appeared on the soundtracks from the films *Boys on the Side, Where Love Goes,* and *Hope Floats,* in which she transforms the Supremes classic "Stop in the Name of Love" into a blistering, heart-wrenching R & B ballad.

We credit Jonell with introducing us to Maura O'Connell, a woman with a voice as lovely as her native Ireland. The two of them perform regular In the Round shows at the cafe. Jonell is also kind enough to lend her talents to all of our Christmas and anniversary benefit shows.

Jonell is now married with two beautiful children. We don't see her as often as we'd like, but we couldn't be happier for her. Unlike Janis Joplin, the soul shouter she's most often compared to, Jonell has managed to keep the ache and the longing in her music while finding some peace and happiness in her life.

Pat Pattison

The Bluebird has been good to me. I've done fifteen lyric-writing workshops there in the past few years, running them on Sundays from ten to four, mostly on weekends when I come down from Boston, where I teach lyric writing and poetry at Berklee College of Music. It's quite an experience teaching songwriting from a stage where many of the planet's best songwriters have been. Pretty humbling. I just try to talk as coherently as possible about what they do and maybe something about how they do it. I'm proud to be there.

The Bluebird is a great feeding hole, too. When I come down summers to write, most evenings will find me there sitting by the window listening, sometimes for an hour, sometimes fifteen minutes. Just to listen to great songs, good songs, or so-so songs. There's always something to inspire you if you pay attention: a chord change, a lick that might be a great springboard for a melody or a bass line, a lyric idea that you take in a totally different direction—all grist for the mill. And you can always find something going on there. For me, the early shows are best. They're usually not filled with writers playing their strings of greatest hits.

Rod Kennedy, founder of the Kerrville Folk Festival in Kerrville, Texas, is joined by fellow Texans (left to right) David Ball and Gary Nicholson.

Every spring break since 1988 I bring about a hundred Berklee students to Nashville for five days of clinics, panels, performances, and tours of studios, publishing houses, and record companies. Nashville rolls out the red carpet, and we've seen the best of everything. The culminating event is a Tuesday-night show at the Bluebird, featuring performances by many of the clinicians they heard from over the weekend at Warner/Reprise (who donate their conference room for the weekend) or at ASCAP, BMI, or SESAC (who donate their conference rooms on weekdays). Quite a list: Beth Nielsen Chapman, Janis Ian, Mike Reid, Gary Burr, Annie Roboff, Gary Nicholson, Bill Lloyd, Rusty Young, Kim Richey, Lari White, Chuck Cannon, Chuck Jones, Steven Allen Davis, Marcus Hummon, Josh Leo, and many more. It's a private affair, only for Berklee, but the shows are the kind you'd need reservations for weeks in advance just to get in the door. The Bluebird is most accommodating, and feeds us well and often.

The Bluebird is a real resource for performers and songwriters, and an important step along the way for many of my students. Gillian Welch and David Rawlings cut their teeth there, working their way through open mikes to three-song slots to the Friday or Saturday late show. All the way to a Grammy nomination. Kami Lyle got both her publishing and recording deals there. What a great place. Kudos to Amy for keeping it that way.

■   ■   ■   ■   ■

Pat Pattison teaches songwriting at the prestigious Berklee School of Music in Boston. He also holds regular songwriting seminars here at the Bluebird.

And finally there's this little flight of fancy from this slightly skewered mind.

Danny Flowers

The Night Marshall Chapman and Jonell Mosser Picked Me Up at the Bar in the Bluebird Cafe

It was a night like any other night. It had signaled the sad end of a day like many other days, one full of rejection in the music business, *my* business. I was at home in my little apartment, decorated with memorabilia of a great career that either never was or was soon to be. I couldn't take it anymore, so I decided to be alone somewhere else, perhaps in a room full of people. I don't remember if it was raining or not; it should have been. I only remember that it was dark. Very dark.

More cheap sunglasses on display with ZZ Top's Billy Gibbons and Marshall Chapman.

Dressed somewhat casually, so as not to call attention or cause distraction, as was the fashion of the day I adjusted my overall straps and sighed deeply as I stared up at the blue-and-white neon sign that simply read THE BLUEBIRD CAFE (mecca for songwriters). I paid my twenty-dollar cover charge and walked in trying only to be recognized by the right people and not the left ones.

The room was full but not packed with people there to hear touchy-feely folk music performed by the people who wrote the songs, mostly in the key of D.

There at the bar was an empty seat right next to Marshall Chapman, my favorite cowriter, dear old friend, and someone that I had always looked up to. We hugged, we sat, we whispered ('cause you can't talk at the Bluebird unless you're paid to do so). We ordered several glasses of dark red wine, none of which we drank. Having given up on drinking and a few other things, we just swished it and spit it out in an empty plastic gallon-sized Purity milk jug and just acted drunk. No one seemed to mind.

For some reason, I told her that in all of my years of bar flying over Nashville I had never been picked up in a bar and had always wondered what that would be like. In that instant, quick as a flash and nimbler than a Santa's helper at the mall, she jumped up, knocked her chair over into a midlevel Music Row executive, spilling his drink, and put her long, steely, muscular arms around me, told me that she loved me, and lifted me right off my chair and held me high up in the air for a full eight seconds, though it seemed much longer at the time. The buzzer went off, and she sat me back down, stood back, smiled, and studied my reaction. I smiled too.

Just then Jonell Mosser walked by. She was the cutest little red-haired blues singer since Howdy Doody and a good friend of everybody's. She had a reputation as one who would never back down from a challenge (either professionally or personally). Not to be outdone, she put down her purse, coat, microphone stand, baby car seat, Jack Daniel's, and marine corps scabbard in the middle of the floor, and tripped a waitress with a full tray of beer. Jonell helped the waitress up, then turned back to me and proceeded to pick me up high in the air, causing Marshall to spew Robert Mondavi all over a table full of really nice people.

Incredible, I thought! Impossible! First of all, Jonell was only four feet twelve, and second of all, she was with another man. Undaunted, and with a low grunt previously only heard in childbirth classes, she picked me up like a flagpole and paraded me from one end of the bar down to Marshall's lap at the other.

The folksingers were now up to the key of E.

Then appeared, as if from somewhere, Amy Kurland, proprietress. She was livid and rather short. I don't know to this day if it was anger or jealousy, but she proceeded to pick me up too! Only with Amy it was with one hand around the back of my delicate neck. She carried me all the way to the front door in one arm, whispering expletive-deleteds and shaking her finger in my face with the other hand. I couldn't breathe! Then with a swift kick she sent me sailing through the parking lot and before I even hit the ground suspended me from coming back in for a full year. She didn't do *nothing* to them.

Needless to say, I went home confused and bruised, but secretly kinda happy that I had finally been picked up in a bar, not once but three times in the same night. Not to mention I had made a name for myself and become a legend at the world-famous Bluebird Cafe.

■ ■ ■ ■ ■

When he's not being picked up in bars, Danny Flowers is known to write classics like "Tulsa Time" and "Back in My Younger Days." He's also been a touring member of Nanci Griffith's Blue Moon Orchestra.

CHAPTER

10 RECIPES

FAVORITE BLUEBIRD RECIPES

You'll recall that when the Bluebird first opened, Amy's mission was to have a first-class restaurant, with music on the weekends. We served lunch and within a month expanded to dinner. Soon the music expanded to seven days a week and the cafe was open eighteen hours a day. The original kitchen staff consisted of Mark Benner and Paula Green cooking and John Ryan handling the desserts. Karen King was our first waitress. Amy watched the books and helped out in the kitchen when necessary.

The kitchen is a tiny one. You have to be on good terms with your coworkers in that little space. There was no automatic dishwasher back then. Dishes were all washed by hand, and finding a good dish-washer was a beautiful thing.

Still, some culinary magic was worked in our little cafe. Restaurant reviewers wrote many glowing articles on the fine cuisine coming from the Bluebird. Here's how it all went down, from one of our first employees.

Mark Benner

The Bluebird has become a world-famous listening room. Amy, the staff, and songwriters deserve a lot of credit, but few people are aware that the truth is that I am responsible for much of the club's success.

When we first opened, the Bluebird really was a cafe, serving lunch and din-ner with music on the weekends. We got reviewed. The style of cuisine de-pended upon the personality of the in-dividual cooks.

Amy had trouble employing cre-ative talent in the kitchen, however, and after a few years the lunches had de-

He's a schoolteacher now but years ago, Mark Benner was our first man in the kitchen.

clined and the wait staff had grown surly. I stopped in one morning about thirty minutes prior to opening for lunch and found Amy in a down mood. She told me that running the place was becoming such a struggle. Cooks calling in sick, storage woes, wear and tear, et cetera. I asked her how much money she was making on lunches, and she said that was the worst part—she was losing money. I suggested she stop doing lunch. She could use all the spare time on booking the club. Amy's face suddenly brightened, she stood up, went back to the kitchen window, and shouted, "Turn everything off! We're clos-ing for lunch!" That quick, it was over. But you know, it worked. Amy suddenly had all that spare time to work on the music, social, and civic activities, and now, of course, the Bluebird is world-famous.

Amy and I have been friends for a long time, all the way back in high school. I helped run her Bakery at Goodies Warehouse, and I learned to cook from Amy's mother, Barbara, on the many evenings that I had dinner with the Kurlands. The one thing, the most important thing, that Barbara taught me, was that in most cooking, precise measurement is not always necessary or desirable. This is something I took to heart and while I followed the same basic format for our regular dishes, I often improvised on the specials. Nowadays, Emeril and others on Food Network advocate a similar approach. If I had my own TV show, it would have to be called *The Cookin' Fool*.

So, you should be adventurous when you cook, especially with stews and soups. Baking is a whole different story.

 ## CREAM OF MUSHROOM SOUP

This can be easily adapted to almost any vegetable. We often do broccoli and asparagus, adjusting seasonings to suit the vegetable.   Serves 8

1 cup butter
1 onion, diced
4 cloves garlic (*more or less, to taste*), minced
1 tablespoon white pepper
2 tablespoons basil
1 tablespoon marjoram
1 tablespoon thyme

1 tablespoon rosemary
8 cups milk
½ cup flour
1 pound or more mushrooms, sliced
⅓ cup red wine
Salt

Melt ¾ cup of butter in a pan, add onion, garlic, and half of the herbs and spices, and sauté until tender. At the same time, slowly heat the milk in a saucepan; do not boil.

Stirring with a whisk, add the flour to the onions and butter and cook over medium heat until you have a nice, consistent roux.

Depending on how good you are at stirring, you can add the roux gradually to the heated milk, whisking to distribute the roux evenly before adding more, or you can do the sissy but safe thing and add the milk gradually to the roux (making sure the roux is cooked in a pan large enough to hold the end result). Continue to heat but do not boil.

While all of this is going on, in a skillet, heat the remaining butter, herbs, and spices, then add the mushrooms and sauté. When the mushrooms are getting soft, add the red wine and continue cooking. When the 'shrooms look done, add them to the butter/milk mixture. Salt to taste.

If using vegetables other than mushrooms, choose your spices and wine accordingly.

 BLACK BEAN SOUP

Frijoles negros are the king of beans. The really great thing about this recipe is that it is very versatile. The longer you cook it, the better it gets. If you reduce the liquid and keep the base thick, you can roll the beans in flour or corn tortillas and top them with cheese like enchiladas or burritos. Puree this recipe and it makes a great black bean dip. This can be served the day it is cooked, but it is at its best consistency and flavor the second day. Remember to buy your beans in advance as you will need to soak them for at least a day before you make this soup.   Serves 12

Olive oil to cover bottom of pan
1 large yellow onion, sliced
   very thin
1 teaspoon basil
1 teaspoon thyme
1 teaspoon chile powder
1 teaspoon cayenne pepper
½ teaspoon coriander
½ teaspoon cumin
½ teaspoon dried mustard powder
8 ounces mushrooms, sliced
3 Anaheim chiles, chopped
   (*You can add more if you
   like it hot.*)
2 banana peppers

5 large cloves garlic,
   chopped coarsely
1 pound ground sausage *(You can
   substitute ground beef, turkey,
   or soy products.)*
½ cup red wine or beer
One 12-ounce bag of dried black
   beans, rinsed and soaked for
   24 hours. Change the water a
   few times while soaking.
4 cups chicken or vegetable stock
Cooked rice *(optional)*
Sour cream *(optional)*
Chopped cilantro or parsley as
   a garnish *(optional)*

Heat the olive oil and add the onions and herbs and spices and stir. Add the mushrooms, and continue to sauté. Add chiles, peppers, garlic, and the sausage, and cook until the meat is browned.

Add the red wine and make sure to scrape all the good browned bits up from the bottom of the pot. Drain the beans and add them to the pot with the stock; bring to a boil. Simmer, covered, stirring occasionally, for at least 2 hours. The longer you simmer, the better it will be. Serve over rice with a dollop of sour cream and a sprinkle of chopped cilantro or parsley.

 SHRIMP GUMBO

The word gumbo *is taken from the African word for "okra." If you are not a Southerner or have never lived in the South, you may not be familiar with this somewhat slimy vegetable that so distinctively thickens whatever you are cooking. We always use lobster stock in our seafood soups, but since it isn't readily available, you can try it with fish or chicken stock.*

The best gumbo we ever had was brought to one of our early Christmas parties, the first or second year we were open. It was a potluck affair, and Dalton Grant, who had been a local high school football star (recruited to the University of Pittsburgh during Dan Marino's days) surprised us all with this amazing gumbo. "How come you didn't tell us you were such a great cook?" we asked. Dalton fessed up and said that in fact his grandmother had made it. Unfortunately, this is my recipe and not Dalton's grandmother's.

Makes 8 hearty portions

¼ cup olive oil
2 cups chopped onions
½ pound ground sausage *(optional)*
5 cloves garlic, chopped
1 tablespoon thyme
2 bay leaves
1 teaspoon dry mustard powder
1 tablespoon file gumbo
½ cup thinly sliced green peppers
½ cup thinly sliced red peppers
½ cup flour

½ cup red wine
2 pounds peeled uncooked shrimp
    *(For crab gumbo, substitute
    crabmeat here. If you prefer
    chicken gumbo, cook it before
    adding to the stew.)*
4 cups chicken or fish stock
2 pounds sliced okra *(You can use
    frozen if you can't get fresh;
    it works very well.)*
Cooked rice

In a large 6-quart saucepan, heat the oil and brown the onions. Add the sausage, garlic, herbs, spices, and peppers and cook over low heat until the sausage is browned and the onions and peppers are soft. Add the flour and stir to create a roux. Add the wine and the shrimp and cook for 1 minute until the shrimp start to turn pink. Add the stock and bring to a boil. Add the okra and reduce the heat to low. Simmer, covered, stirring occasionally, for 30 minutes and serve over rice.

Desserts

At the Bluebird we made two wonderful cakes that everyone loved. Our pastry chef John Ryan taught us to make genoise (sponge) cakes the French way, beating the eggs over heat as you add the flour, but we suggest you use your best sponge cake recipe for these cakes. Bake one large 10-inch layer and cool thoroughly in the refrigerator. If you use a box mix, bake it all in the large pan. You need a tall cake in order to slice it into three layers.

 ## GÂTEAU DE PAQUE—LEMON RASPBERRY CAKE

This recipe is layers of cake flavored with simple syrup, raspberry jam, and lemony cream cheese icing. Use a yellow or white cake recipe. The simple syrup recipe makes much more than you will need; keep it in the refrigerator for next time.

SIMPLE SYRUP

½ gallon water	2½ pounds sugar

CREAM CHEESE ICING

1½ pounds cream cheese, softened slightly	Juice of 2 large lemons
	1 cup confectioners' sugar
One 10-inch yellow or white sponge cake	Raspberry jam *(Get the best; it's worth it.)*

Make the simple syrup. Bring the water to a boil and add the sugar, stirring until all the crystals are dissolved. Cool. Add flavoring as desired; Amaretto or Grand Marnier would be great for this cake. Set aside; we kept our simple syrup in a bottle with a nice pour spout.

Make the cream cheese icing: Beat all ingredients together until smooth. Set aside.

Remove the cake from the pan and slice it horizontally into thirds so that you end up with three layers. Place the bottom layer onto a cardboard cake round or cake plate. Wet the cake with the simple syrup. Use liberally, but don't get the cake soggy. Spread on a ¼-inch layer of the cream cheese icing followed by a thin coating of the raspberry jam. Place the middle cake layer on and repeat with syrup, icing, and jam. Holding the top layer of cake, sliced side up, wet that layer with syrup also. Place on top and ice the cake top and sides. We use a cake comb to make grooved sides, and put the remaining icing in a pastry bag to decorate the cake.

 ## BLACK FOREST CAKE

For the black forest cake, we start with a chocolate sponge cake and layer it with simple syrup, chocolate custard, canned black cherries, and whipped cream. It doesn't last long, but it's great.

CHOCOLATE CUSTARD

4 tablespoons flour	8 egg yolks
2 cups light cream	2 teaspoons vanilla
¼ teaspoon salt	8 ounces unsweetened chocolate,
¾ cup sugar	chopped coarsely

WHIPPED CREAM ICING

2 cups heavy cream	½ cup confectioners' sugar

One 10-inch chocolate sponge cake	Simple Syrup *(page 163)*,
1 can black cherries, drained	flavored with kirsch

Make the custard: In a medium saucepan, combine the flour with a small amount of the cream and whisk thoroughly to combine; keep the lumps out. Then add the remaining cream, salt, and sugar and heat on low, stirring constantly until thickened. Remove from the heat and add the egg yolks and vanilla, continuing to stir until thickened. Add the chocolate and stir until melted. Cool in the refrigerator.

Make the whipped cream icing: Whip the heavy cream and confectioners' sugar until thick.

Remove the cake from the pan and slice it horizontally into thirds so that you end up with three layers. Place the bottom layer onto a cardboard cake round or cake plate. Wet the cake with the simple syrup. Use liberally, but don't get the cake soggy. Spread on half of the chocolate custard, cover it with half the cherries in a single layer, and add a layer of about one-fourth the whipped cream icing. Place the middle cake layer on top and repeat with syrup, custard, cherries, and whipped cream.

Holding the top layer of cake, sliced side up, wet that layer with syrup also. Place on top and ice the cake top and sides with the remaining whipped cream. Decorate the cake with grated chocolate and extra cherries, if desired.

CHOCOLATE RASPBERRY CAKE

This creation by Mark Benner calls for chocolate whipped cream. Once you have made this, you may never go back to plain whipped cream again.

CHOCOLATE WHIPPED CREAM

8 ounces semisweet chocolate	¼ cup confectioners' sugar
1 quart heavy whipping cream	Vanilla to taste

One 10-inch chocolate sponge cake	Raspberry jam
Simple Syrup *(page 163)*	Chocolate Custard *(page 164)*

Make the chocolate whipped cream: Melt the chocolate in the top of a double boiler. Remove from the heat and let cool slightly. Stir into the whipping cream and cool in the refrigerator until quite cold. Whip this chocolate cream with the confectioners' sugar and vanilla until it is a thick whipped cream consistency.

Remove the cake from the pan and slice it horizontally into thirds so that you end up with three layers. Place bottom layer onto a cardboard cake round or cake plate. Wet the cake with the simple syrup. Use liberally, but don't get the cake soggy. Spread on a ¼-inch layer of raspberry jam, followed by half of the chocolate custard, and add a layer about one-fourth of the chocolate whipped cream. Place the middle cake layer on top and repeat with syrup, jam, custard, and whipped cream. Holding the top layer of cake, sliced side up, wet that layer with syrup also. Place on top and ice the cake the top and sides with the remaining whipped cream. Decorate the cake with grated chocolate and fresh raspberries, if desired.

CHAMBORD CHOCOLATE MOUSSE

John Ryan established a tradition of placing the mousse in regular eight-ounce water glasses, downplaying a very elegant dessert. He did a regular chocolate and a Chambord (raspberry liqueur)-flavored chocolate version. When Mark took over doing the desserts, he experimented further, adding white chocolate or Cointreau to make an orange-chocolate mousse. The possibilities are endless, but be careful melting rogue elements with the chocolate, and avoid getting water in it.

We scoop the mousse into pastry bags and squeeze it into the glasses, topping them off with a dollop of whipped cream and a mint leaf. You have to be careful to not handle the mousse too roughly, or you'll break the air bubbles in the egg whites and the mousse will become runny. Heat is bad too, and on some Nashville nights, when the natural high temperature and humidity of the town combine with the heat of the Bluebird oven, it's impossible to make mousse. This was a task Mark often reserved for early morning or as an excuse to stay late and listen to the music. Serves 12 to 15

18 ounces semisweet chocolate, chopped
2 cups heavy cream, very cold
½ cup granulated sugar
6 eggs, separated
3 tablespoons Chambord (raspberry liqueur)
1 teaspoon vanilla

Melt the chocolate in the top of a double boiler. Let cool to just warm.

Whip the cream with ¼ cup of the sugar until it forms medium peaks.

In a large bowl, beat the egg yolks until thick and lemon-colored. Add the melted chocolate, half of the whipped cream, and the Chambord and vanilla and fold together until smooth.

In another, very clean large bowl, whip the egg whites until they are frothy, add the remaining sugar, and whip to firm peaks. Gently fold in the egg yolk–chocolate mixture and the remaining whipped cream. Don't overdo this, you want to keep as much air in it as possible.

Scoop the mousse into a large pastry bag and pipe it into brandy snifters. Refrigerate for at least 4 hours. Garnish with additional whipped cream and a mint leaf or a fresh raspberry.

CHOCOLATE CHUNK CHEESECAKE

We have been serving this recipe for eighteen years, and it's still very popular. One really needs a good French knife or even a cleaver to chop the chocolate into coarse chunks. We used to get our chocolate in ten-pound bars from the Bluebell Chocolate Company in Louisville, Kentucky. Serves 14

GRAHAM CRACKER CRUST

2 cups graham cracker crumbs	1 teaspoon cinnamon
¾ stick melted butter	

CHEESECAKE

1½ pounds cream cheese	2 tablespoons vanilla
Scant 1 cup granulated sugar	½ cup half-and-half
6 tablespoons cornstarch	1½ cups coarsely chopped
4 extra-large eggs	semisweet chocolate

Combine crust ingredients and stir until evenly blended. Pack into the bottom of a 10-inch springform pan.

Preheat the oven to 250°F.

Put the cream cheese, sugar, and cornstarch in the bowl of an electric mixer and blend on low until combined. Add the eggs one at a time, mixing between each one. Add the vanilla and half-and-half and mix until blended.

Spread 1¼ cups of the chocolate in the graham cracker crust. Pour the batter over it and sprinkle the remaining chocolate on top. Bake for 1 hour and 40 minutes until firm. Turn off the heat and let sit in oven for another 15 minutes. Cool on a cake rack for at least an hour, before moving into the refrigerator.

Celebrity Recipes

Contrary to popular opinion, many artists and songwriters know how to cook more than Kraft macaroni and cheese. Creating a beautiful dish and creating a beautiful song have much in common. You need to have the right ingredients, know how to put them together and just how long to let it all cook. Whether you're in the mood for something sweet or something sizzling, the right song and the right dish are always a joy to experience. We suggest you put on a favorite from your musical menu while you whip up one of these wonderful recipes from our Bluebird family of friends.

 ## AMY GRANT'S CHEESE GRITS

This recipe was prepared by Grandma Grant and has been passed down to our family. It's one of my favorites.   **Serves 4**

4 cups water
1 teaspoon salt
1 cup grits
1 wheel garlic cheese *(about
    5 ounces, like Boursin)*

1 stick butter
2 eggs
Milk
Cheddar cheese, grated *(optional)*
Paprika

Preheat the oven to 325°F. Bring the water to a boil in a medium saucepan. Add the salt and grits and cook until you get a soupy texture. Remove from heat, and add the garlic cheese and butter. Stir. Crack the eggs into a large measuring cup, and add enough milk to make 1 cup. Beat the eggs and milk lightly and add it to the grits.

Pour into a greased baking dish. Cover the grits with the cheddar, if desired. Sprinkle generously with paprika. Bake for 30 to 40 minutes.

RUSTY YOUNG'S
POCO TORTILLA SOUP

Serves 8

2 tablespoons olive oil
6 yellow onions, chopped
1 carrot, diced
4 cloves garlic, minced
Red and yellow peppers, diced
6 cups chicken stock

Cilantro
Dash of lemon juice
3 chicken breasts
Tortilla chips
Sour cream
Green onions, diced

Heat the olive oil. Sauté the onions with the carrot, garlic, and half each of the peppers. Simmer about 30 minutes, then add the stock and cilantro (to taste) with the lemon juice. Continue to simmer.

Next, grill the chicken breasts and dice them. Finally, spoon the soup into bowls, add the grilled chicken, and set the tortilla chips around the soup bowls. Garnish with a dollop of sour cream and the diced green onion.

Enjoy.

P.S. Dos Equis is the recommended beverage.

KENYA WALKER'S WISH SALAD

This is my own personal simple taste, but you can make your own wish salad by ONLY using ingredients that you LOVE and leaving everything that you just can't tolerate in a salad OUT. First my wish salad only has lettuce in it if it is fresh tender Boston lettuce—I hate nasty iceberg. Boston is my favorite for this because its flavor doesn't interfere with all the other flavors. (It works great without lettuce too.) As I make the salad, I name and bless each ingredient to nurture and heal the body, mind, and soul of the person or persons who the salad is meant for. For example, black olives would represent a rich abundance of wisdom in life experience to come to the eater of the salad. Tomatoes would represent passion to be restored in the lives of the those who have lost their passion for their work or for living. I name what each ingredient represents according to who will be partaking of the salad. I make uplifting wishes for those who eat the salad, a salad made of love and wishes—thus wish salad.

These are my favorite ingredients:

Artichoke hearts—1 jar
Bell pepper—green, orange,
  or red, whatever your taste
Black olives—1 can drained
  small or medium
Boston lettuce
1 carrot, sliced or grated,
  whatever your taste
Chickpeas *(garbanzo beans)*,
  1 can, drained

Hard-boiled eggs, 4 to 6
Fresh tomatoes, as many
  as you want
Onions—mild, sweet-flavored
Dressing—only your favorite—
  mine is ranch, made with
  plain milk from the little
  package from Hidden
  Valley

Arrange and layer the salad as you want; it is a personal dish meant to satisfy your own desires.

ROBERTO BIANCO'S ROMANTIC SQUASH

My recipe for romance is one that I have used in each of my marriages, or whenever the occasion arose.

Cut up a lot of yellow squash into thin slices. Steam until soft. Put into a warm bowl, and stir in a commensurate amount of Philadelphia cream cheese and some chives to taste. This warm and delicious concoction will be loved by young and old as an entrée or a side dish and is a delightful way to awaken a sensual moment.

MOM PISTILLI'S ARTICHOKES

1. Find beautiful artichokes (1 per person).
2. Cut off the points with scissors or a knife.
3. Cut off the bottoms so they can stand flat in a pot; keep the stems.
4. Turn the artichokes upside down, and rub the leaves back and forth on the counter to help open them up. Open the leaves as wide as possible.
5. Over a large bowl, fill all openings as much as you can with Italian-style bread crumbs.
6. Heat enough olive oil in the bottom of a pot large enough to hold the artichokes in one layer.
7. Stand the artichokes in the pot, and brown the bottoms for a minute or two.
8. Add wine to fill the pot about ½ inch, cover, and steam for at least 2 hours. As the liquid boils away, add water to maintain the level of liquid.
9. Baste the artichokes with the cooking liquid every half hour or so. The longer these cook, the better they taste.

BETH NIELSEN CHAPMAN'S
WEST INDIES SALAD

You can make it the night before and it's amazing the next day. This is very simple but really good! Serve by placing a small scoopful onto a single leaf of Bibb or romaine lettuce per person.   Serves 4 as an appetizer

1 medium-large onion,
   finely chopped
1 pound fresh lump crabmeat
½ cup Wesson oil *(has to be Wesson)*

½ cup apple cider vinegar
½ cup ice water
Salt and pepper to taste

   In a shallow dish, spread the chopped onion in an even layer. Lovingly and carefully layer the lump crabmeat on top so as to preserve as much "lumpage" as possible. Combine the other ingredients in a small bowl, and pour over the onion and crab. Cover and marinate in the refrigerator for at least 8 hours.

DIXIE CHICK EMILY ERWIN'S
BISTRO **CHICK**EN PASTA SALAD

Serves 4

2 cups cooked rotini

1 cup quartered cherry tomatoes

4 ounces feta cheese, crumbled,
  or cheddar, cubed

½ cup prepared honey mustard
  or Caesar salad dressing

⅓ cup lightly packed fresh
  basil leaves, cut into strips

¼ cup chopped red onion

¼ cup sun-dried tomatoes packed
  in oil, drained and chopped

¼ teaspoon pepper

2 boneless skinless chicken breast
  halves, grilled or broiled,
  cut into ¼-inch slices

Mix all the ingredients except the chicken. Top pasta mixture with chicken. Serve warm or chilled.

KIMMIE RHODES'S BABETTE'S EGGPLANT GRATIN

This dish is usually served in single portions as a starter course, but it's also good as a main course with fettuccine on the side and a grating of fresh Parmesan on top. If done correctly it will be very thin and light. The eggplant should be sliced thinly, which prevents it from soaking up too much oil and gives the dish its wonderful delicateness. This is the secret to the dish.

Serves 8 as a first course

1 head garlic
One 28-ounce can crushed tomatoes
1 large eggplant
Olive oil

8 ounces Gruyère cheese, grated
1½ cups bread crumbs
Salt and pepper

Peel and chop the entire head of garlic. Put the garlic and tomatoes in a saucepan and cook slowly, uncovered, for about 1 hour, until the sauce is thick.

Preheat the oven to 400°F.

Wash the eggplant and slice thinly (about ⅛ inch). Sauté the eggplant slices in olive oil until tender. Drain on paper towels.

Line a large, shallow casserole dish with a layer of the cooked eggplant slices. Spread a thin layer of the thickened tomato sauce on top of that, and top that with a layer of grated cheese. Repeat these layers one more time, then end with a generous layer of bread crumbs.

Bake for about 45 minutes or until the whole casserole bubbles and the bread-crumb topping is crusty and dark golden brown.

Season with salt and pepper.

BILLY KIRSCH'S ZITI AND SPINACH PARMESAN

When my wife, Julie, was undergoing cancer treatment, our friends organized a dinner drop-off that lasted many nights. Every other night friends knocked on our front door with a wonderful homemade meal for us. This is my favorite of all the dishes brought to us. Now we take it to other friends when they need a great meal.   Serves 4 to 6

2 tablespoons extra-virgin olive oil
1 medium onion, coarsely chopped
3 medium garlic cloves, finely chopped
One 28-ounce can Italian whole peeled tomatoes
¼ teaspoon crushed red pepper flakes
¾ teaspoon salt
¼ teaspoon freshly ground black pepper

10 ounces ziti *(about 3 cups)*, uncooked
1 pound fresh spinach, stems discarded, leaves thoroughly rinsed, dried, and coarsely chopped
6 ounces *(about 1 cup)* part-skim mozzarella cheese, cut into ½-inch dice
1 cup freshly grated Parmesan cheese

1. Heat the oil in a large, nonreactive skillet, then sauté the onion and garlic over moderate heat until the onion is soft, about 5 minutes. Using your hands, break up the tomatoes and add them with their juice to the skillet. Stir in the crushed red pepper. Increase the heat to moderately high, and bring to a boil, stirring. Add salt and pepper. Lower the heat and keep warm.
2. Preheat the broiler. Meanwhile, bring a large pot of salted water to a boil and cook the ziti until al dente, 9 to 11 minutes. Drain well and return to the pot. Stir in the spinach, mozzarella, and ⅓ cup of the Parmesan. Add the tomato sauce and toss.
3. Transfer the ziti to a shallow 14-inch oval gratin dish (9 x 13-inch works too), and sprinkle the remaining ⅔ cup Parmesan on top. Broil 1 to 2 minutes, until browned.

JOY LYNN WHITE'S
WHITE CLAM SAUCE FOR PASTA

Serves 2

Pasta for two

4 tablespoons chopped onion

2 garlic cloves, minced

2 tablespoons olive oil

1 teaspoon lemon juice

4 tablespoons white wine

1 teaspoon thyme

¼ teaspoon crushed red pepper flakes

One 6.5-ounce can chopped clams
  with juice

2 tablespoons fresh basil

2 tablespoons chopped fresh
  parsley

Grated Parmesan cheese

While cooking the pasta, sauté the onion and garlic in olive oil. Add the lemon juice, wine, thyme, and pepper flakes. Heat slowly. After draining the pasta, add it along with clams, clam juice, basil, and parsley to the sauce. Allow the pasta to absorb the juices a few minutes. Toss and garnish with grated Parmesan.

GENE PISTILLI'S BULLETPROOF SPAGHETTI SAUCE AND MEATBALLS

This is not so much my sauce as one that has evolved over the years. It's a very basic recipe, but for some reason it has been pleasing the troops I've served it to for over twenty-five years. It passes through me to you with much love and tenderness from three chubby angels: my grandmother, Regina Santoro; my mom, Mary; and my dear friend George Memoli. So the next time you start browning onions and garlic in olive oil and the fragrance drifts through your kitchen (especially on a Sunday morning), there will be smiles on the faces of three residents of Heaven's Italian neighborhood. Serves 8

1 cup olive oil
1 onion, chopped
4 cloves garlic, chopped
Two 28-ounce cans tomato puree
  (*I use Progresso*)
One 28-ounce can crushed plum
  tomatoes
3 cans tomato paste
Pork neck bones *(optional)*

1 tablespoon oregano
1 tablespoon basil
1 tablespoon salt
½ teaspoon black pepper
3 cups water
1 cup red wine
Grated Parmesan cheese
1 tablespoon sugar

MEATBALLS

2 pounds ground chuck
2 eggs
6 thick slices sourdough bread
  moistened with red wine
1 onion, chopped
Grated Parmesan cheese

Marjoram
Oregano
Fresh chopped parsley
Garlic powder
Salt and pepper

Prepare the sauce: Heat the olive oil and brown the onion and garlic. Add the tomato puree, crushed tomatoes, and tomato paste. If using pork neck bones for flavor, add them now. Add the herbs, salt, pepper, water, wine, a handful or cheese, and the sugar and simmer for 4 hours.

Prepare the meatballs: Mix together the ground chuck, eggs, moistened bread, onion, and a handful of cheese. Season liberally with the herbs, garlic powder, salt, and pepper. Cook a little bit of the meat in a small pan to check the seasonings.

Form 2-inch meatballs and add them raw to the sauce about 30 minutes before you're ready to serve. They will be cooked and fluffy.

ASHLEY CLEVELAND'S
CHILAQUILE CON POLLO

Serves 6 to 8

2 pounds chicken breasts or thighs
2 medium onions, cut in chunks
1 medium carrot, thickly sliced
1 celery stalk, thickly sliced
1 bay leaf
Salt and pepper to taste
One 7-ounce can green chilis,
    seeded *(or unseeded if a*
    hotter flavor is desired)
12 to 16 ounces tomatillos
    (Mexican green tomatoes,
    available in Mexican groceries
    and specialty stores)

2 garlic cloves, peeled
¼ cup firmly packed cilantro
3 tablespoons lard or vegetable
    shortening
1 cup rich chicken stock
12 corn tortillas,
    cut in strips
Vegetable shortening, as needed,
    for frying
1 to 1½ pounds Monterey Jack
    cheese, grated
Avocado slices
Salsa *(page 179)*

Poach the chicken with 1 onion, carrot, celery, bay leaf, salt, and pepper in water to cover, until tender. When cool enough to handle, bone the chicken and cut into bite-sized pieces. Set aside.

In a blender or food processor, purée the chilis, tomatillos, the remaining onion, garlic, and cilantro. Melt the 3 tablespoons shortening in a heavy skillet, then add the purée. Cook and stir for about 5 minutes. Gradually stir in the chicken stock. Heat through, and adjust salt and pepper.

Quickly fry the tortilla strips in hot lard until just crisp but not brown. Drain on paper towels.

In a buttered 8 x 12-inch shallow baking dish, layer the tortillas, chicken, cheese, and sauce. Repeat until all the ingredients are used, reserving enough cheese to sprinkle on top. Cover and refrigerate for 8 hours or overnight. Bake, uncovered, in a preheated 350°F oven for 45 minutes or until heated through and cheese is melted. Garnish with avocado slices, and serve with salsa.

 ## SALSA

Makes 3 cups

4 small tomatoes, peeled, seeded, and chopped	One 8-ounce can tomato sauce
½ cup chopped onion	1 teaspoon salt
½ cup finely chopped bell pepper	½ teaspoon coriander
2 jalapeño peppers, minced	½ teaspoon oregano
1 tablespoon white vinegar	2 tablespoons oil
1 tablespoon sugar	1 tablespoon lemon or lime juice

Combine all the ingredients. Cover and refrigerate for several hours.

 ## DIXIE CHICK NATALIE MAINES'S OVEN-BARBECUED HAWAIIAN **CHICK**EN

Serves 4

One 8-ounce can crushed pineapple in unsweetened pineapple juice	2 tablespoons soy sauce
⅓ cup chili sauce	1 teaspoon cornstarch
¼ cup apricot preserves	3½-pound broiler-fryer, cut up
2 tablespoons brown sugar	1 medium-sized pineapple
	Lettuce leaves for garnish (*optional*)

Preheat oven to 400°F. In a small bowl, combine the crushed pineapple with its juice, chili sauce, apricot preserves, brown sugar, soy sauce, and cornstarch; mix well.

Remove the skin and fat from all the chicken pieces except the wings. Arrange the chicken in 15½ x 10½-inch roasting pan lined with foil. Spoon the pineapple mixture over the chicken.

Bake for 45 to 50 minutes, basting occasionally with the pan drippings, until juices run clear when the chicken is pierced with a knife.

While the chicken is cooking, cut off the crown and stem of the pineapple; trim off the rind. Cut the pineapple lengthwise into quarters. Cut each quarter crosswise into ¾-inch-thick slices.

Arrange the chicken and pineapple on a large platter. Garnish with lettuce leaves if you like. Spoon any sauce left in the roasting pan over chicken.

Total time: 1¼ hours

Each serving without pineapple: about 345 calories, 5 grams fat, 119 milligrams cholesterol, 955 milligrams sodium

179

DIXIE CHICK MARTIE SEIDEL'S
SALSA COUSCOUS **CHICK**EN

Serves 4

3 cups hot cooked couscous or rice
1 tablespoon olive or vegetable oil
¼ cup coarsely chopped almonds
2 garlic cloves, minced
8 chicken thighs, skin removed
1 cup thick-and-chunky salsa

¼ cup water
2 tablespoons dried currants
1 tablespoon honey
¾ teaspoon cumin
½ teaspoon cinnamon

While the couscous is cooking, heat the oil in a large skillet over medium-high heat. Add the almonds; cook 1 to 2 minutes or until golden brown. Remove the almonds from the skillet with a slotted spoon, and set aside.

Add the garlic to the skillet and stir for 30 seconds. Add the chicken and cook 4 to 5 minutes or until browned, turning once.

In a medium bowl, combine the salsa with the water, currants, honey, cumin, and cinnamon; mix well. Add to the chicken; mix well. Reduce heat to medium, cover, and cook stirring occasionally, for 20 minutes or until the chicken is fork-tender and the juices run clear. Stir in the almonds. Serve with couscous.

Prep time: 30 minutes

BOBBY ROSS'S
LIME-BAKED CHICKEN

This is a very simple recipe, and it was a big hit when I used to cook at the Bluebird. Also, it's very generous on the songwriter's pocketbook. And it goes with just about anything.　　　　　　　　　　　　　Serves 2 comfortably

1 average-sized whole chicken	Celery salt
Salt	Paprika
Pepper	4 limes, cut in half
Garlic salt	

Preheat the oven to at least 375°F. Wash the chicken and shake off excess liquids. Cut the bird in half, and lay both sides in a shallow pan or casserole.

Season to taste, being sure to sprinkle freely both on the outside and the inside of the bird. (To really liven it up, you can stick several types of fresh herbs, whole and expensive, in the bird's cavity.) Lightly squeeze the lime halves over the bird, then place them facedown around it.

Cook for approximately 35 to 45 minutes, depending upon how well-done you like it.

JOHN SCOTT SHERRILL'S
FAMOUS WICKER WINGS

I'm not much of a cook, but I do have one dish for which I am well-known. For the first time I am prepared to share the secret of John Scott's Famous Wicker Wings.

Buy Wicker's barbecue sauce. That's the first part. It should be easy—most stores in the mid-South carry it. It's a vinegar-and-pepper-based sauce, as opposed to tomato-and-sugar-based. While you're at the store, pick up a bunch (I mean a lot—they cook down, and they're really good) of chicken wings. Soak the wings in big saucepans full of Wicker's for 4 or 5 hours (you can parboil them a little in the Wicker's first). Build a hot charcoal fire and spread the wings evenly and tightly across the grill with tongs. This is the hot part and you must work quickly, turning them often enough so they crisp without burning. Baste with Wicker's if they flare up (the vinegar tends to put the fire out, whereas the tomato-and-sugar sauce makes it roar hot). When the wings are nicely browned, baste well and cover the grill tightly. Cook for 45 minutes or so, basting and turning as needed to keep the fire low (but not out) and the wings browning but not soggy. When done, these little tidbits will be crispy on the outside and fall-off-the-bone tender on the inside.

Mmm . . . it's been a while since I made a batch.

JENNIFER KIMBALL AND
RANGER BOB'S SAUTÉED QUAIL

Serves 4

8 quail *(2 per person)*   Freshly ground pepper
Garlic powder   1 stick butter
2 teaspoons rosemary   Flour
Salt   ¼ cup brandy or cognac

Rinse the birds, then pat dry with paper towels. Rub with garlic powder. Crush the rosemary in your palms and rub on the birds. Lightly sprinkle with salt and pepper. Melt the butter in a large skillet. Sprinkle flour on the quail, and place immediately in the skillet. Brown about 3 minutes on each side. Lower the heat and continue cooking until done. Do not overcook. Remove the skillet from the heat, and allow to cool for about 2 minutes. Pour warmed brandy over the birds, flame with a match, and baste with the flaming liquid until flame dies.

JEFFREY STEELE'S
"DAD'S DOGS"

My best-liked recipe is one I started making when I was a kid. Tired of Hamburger Helper and Shake and Bake chicken, my mom gave me cooking duties every Thursday night, and I quickly wowed them all with this simple to make ol' favorite. It's carried on now in my family, whenever we're in a hurry to make lunch or if I get a wild hair to whip 'em up. They're called simply "Dad's dogs."   Serves 4

4 kosher all-beef frankfurters   4 hamburger buns
1 bottle Worcestershire sauce   1 cup grated sharp cheddar cheese
1 jar barbecue sauce

Slice the dogs down the center and place them in a large skillet. Cook over medium heat until they start to brown, not burn, about 2 minutes. Pour in the Worcestershire sauce and turn on the fan, 'cause it will smoke a little. Then coat with barbecue sauce. Flip the dogs to coat them. Then cut them in half so they look like little fingers. Place 4 pieces (1 dog) on each hamburger bun, and add cheese. It's that simple, folks. I like to serve with guacamole and chips and a big iced tea. Cooking time about 7 minutes.

KACEY JONES'S BARBECUE
COUNTRY-STYLE RIBS

I chose this recipe because it's dangerous, delightful, fattening, and finger-lickin' good, just like me!   Serves 4

2 racks country-style beef ribs
Flour
¼ cup vegetable oil
1 cup catsup
1 cup water
2 teaspoons salt

2 tablespoons Worcestershire sauce
½ cup white vinegar
¼ cup brown sugar
2 teaspoons dry mustard
1 cup sliced onions

Dust the ribs with flour. Heat the oil and brown the ribs in a frying pan. Drain off the fat. Combine all the other ingredients in a large pot or Dutch oven. Add the ribs and and simmer for about an hour and a half. Serve with rice, salad, corn on the cob, and lots and lots of napkins.

FROGMORE STEW,
RICHARD LEIGH–STYLE

This is a dish to be cooked and eaten outdoors. It's messy and great. You'll need a large (20-gallon) pot with a strainer insert and an outdoor propane burner. Use whatever seafood is available and fresh. Serve with lots of garlic bread.   Serves 30

4 pounds hot Italian sausage,
   cut into 1½-inch pieces
4 pounds mild Italian sausage,
   cut into 1½-inch pieces
30 medium Vidalia onions, chopped
Two 6-ounce boxes Chesapeake
   Bay Seafood Seasoning
10 pounds new potatoes

30 ears corn, broken into
   3 pieces each
6 pounds shrimp
4 pounds crab legs
9 pounds clams
9 pounds mussels
2 pounds butter, melted

Fill a large pot halfway with water and bring it to a boil, then add the sausage, onions, and a box of the seasoning. Simmer for 45 minutes.

Add the potatoes and boil for 15 minutes. Add the corn and the other box of seasoning, and let boil for 10 minutes more. Add all the seafood and let it steam with the lid on for 10 minutes.

Pull out the strainer and let the water drain back into the pot. Warning: Use an oven mitt; it's going to be really hot. Dump the food onto a cloth-covered picnic table.

Have bowls of melted butter around for dipping!

CHILI SHACK
CHILI BASIC

1 tablespoon oil	One #10 can diced tomatoes
2 large onions, diced	One #10 can cooked pinto beans
2 bell peppers, diced	¼ cup chili powder
5 pounds ground meat	Salt and pepper to taste

Heat one large skillet over medium-high heat. Add the oil, and when it is hot, put in your onions and peppers and cook until soft. Add the ground meat and continue cooking till browned completely. Add the tomatoes, beans, and chili powder. Let simmer as long as you want, add the salt and pepper, and nothing else if Amy Kurland is anywhere around.

Hope the band doesn't play a third set.

CHILI SHACK
CHILI VERSION 4.20

3 cups red wine

1 bottle dark beer

2 tablespoons dry mustard

2 tablespoons coarsely chopped
garlic

2 tablespoons sesame oil

2 oranges, roughly chopped

5 pounds red meat cut into strips
1 inch wide by 1 to 5 inches long

3 pounds fresh tomatoes, seeded
(reserve seeds)

3 large red onions

3 poblano peppers

1 pound portobello mushrooms
*(porto stems are perfect if you
have a lot saved up)*

2 tablespoons fresh minced
garlic

3 cups black beans,
soaked, cooked, and
rinsed—should yield
approximately, 6 cups

3 hot peppers, minced
*(your choice and strictly
optional)*

¼ cup chili powder

2 tablespoons paprika

2 tablespoons Worcestershire
sauce

2 tablespoons soy sauce

Salt and pepper to taste

Mix the wine, beer, mustard, chopped garlic, sesame oil, and oranges in a large bowl. Add the strips of meat, and let marinate overnight. Remove from the liquid and allow to drain.

Either grill and or smoke the meat till medium well. Set aside to cool.

Strain your remaining marinade and in a pot add the seeds from the tomatoes and reduce down to approximately ¼ cup. Strain again and set aside.

In a large cast-iron skillet, sweat your onions, peppers, mushrooms, and minced garlic till the onions are almost translucent. Add the tomatoes and continue to cook over medium heat. Next add your reduced liquid and allow it to deglaze your skillet. Dice the cooked meat, and add it to the skillet along with the beans. Add the remaining ingredients, and simmer for at least an hour. If you desire a thicker chili, you may add tomato paste with the diced tomatoes. As with all chili, this is best if you make it a day ahead and let the flavors marry overnight. Enjoy!

Desserts

 FAITH HILL'S
COCA-COLA CAKE

2 cups unsifted flour
2 cups sugar
2 sticks butter
2 tablespoons cocoa
1 cup Coca-Cola

½ cup buttermilk
1 teaspoon baking soda
2 eggs, beaten
1 teaspoon vanilla
1½ cups miniature marshmallows

ICING

½ cup butter
3 tablespoons cocoa

6 tablespoons Coca-Cola
1 box confectioners' sugar

Preheat the oven to 350°F.

Make the cake: Sift the flour and the sugar in a large bowl.

In a small saucepan, heat the butter, cocoa, and Coke to the boiling point, then pour over the flour mixture.

Add the buttermilk, baking soda, eggs, vanilla, and marshmallows. The batter will be thin, and the marshmallows will float to the top.

Pour the batter into a greased and floured 9 x 13-inch pan, and bake for 30 to 35 minutes. Ice the cake while it's still hot.

Make the icing: Combine the first 3 ingredients in a saucepan. Heat to boiling. Pour over the confectioners' sugar and beat well. Pour over the cake while it's still hot.

LULA'S CHOCOLATE MERINGUE PIE

This is best if eaten the day you make it. As if there would be any left! Note Fran's story on page 103.

1½ cups sugar
3 heaping tablespoons cocoa
3 heaping tablespoons flour
1½ cups whole milk
3 egg yolks *(save the whites for the meringue)*

¼ cup butter
1 teaspoon vanilla
One 8-inch pie crust shell, baked

MERINGUE

3 to 4 egg whites
1 teaspoon cream of tartar

8 tablespoons sugar
1 teaspoon vanilla

Make the pie: Mix the sugar, cocoa, and flour in a medium saucepan. In a separate saucepan, heat the milk until scalding. Slowly pour into the dry-ingredient mixture.

Cook entire mixture over medium heat, stirring constantly, until boiling; about 4 minutes.

Remove from heat and beat in the egg yolks. Return to the stove and cook until thick, stirring constantly, about 2 minutes.

Remove from the heat and add the butter and vanilla. Pour into the baked pie shell.

Make the meringue: Using a mixer, beat the egg whites with the cream of tartar only until they make soft peaks. Gradually add the sugar.

Add the vanilla. Beat until the meringue is stiff and glossy, about 4 to 5 minutes.

Top the pie with meringue. Bake in a preheated 350°F oven until the meringue is brown, approximately 12 to 15 minutes.

FAYE'S ICE CREAM PIE

The pie is great as is, but get creative using other flavors.

One 6-ounce Oreo pie crust
  (no substitute)
2 squares semisweet chocolate
½ cup sugar

1 tablespoon butter or margarine
⅔ cup evaporated milk
½ gallon vanilla ice cream
  (or flavor of your choice)

Freeze the Oreo pie crust.

In the top of a double boiler, melt the chocolate over hot water. Stir in the sugar and the butter or margarine. Add the evaporated milk. Cook until thick, about 10 to 12 minutes, stirring the whole time. Cool and chill.

Set out the ice cream for 10 to 15 minutes until it softens. Fill the pie crust with ice cream. Place in freezer until the ice cream hardens again, about 1 hour.

Spread the chocolate mixture over the top. Freeze again.

When you slice the pie, warm the knife first by running it under hot water.

NANNETTE CLARK'S RED VELVET CAKE

Here is my favorite cake recipe. Actually, it is my mother's recipe. It's been in my family since the early 1960s and traditionally is made for birthdays and holidays. Everyone always fights over the last piece. When we were little, Mother had a little single-serving cake pan and made us individual cakes for our birthdays. These were always the best—better than the big cakes, at least we always thought so. Mother tried using green food coloring for St. Patrick's Day or Christmas, but my brothers and dad insisted it wasn't as good as the red. Silly men. Many friends and relatives have tried to improve on the recipe by using butter and other ingredients, but so far this is the best—with all the sugar, fat, and calories.

1½ cups sugar
½ cup vegetable shortening
2 large eggs
2¼ cups flour
1 tablespoon unsweetened cocoa
1 teaspoon salt

1 cup buttermilk
2 teaspoons vanilla
2 ounces red food coloring
1 teaspoon baking soda
1 tablespoon white vinegar

ICING

¼ cup Betty Crocker Wonder flour
1 cup whole milk
1 cup vegetable shortening

1 cup sugar
1 teaspoon vanilla
Sweetened flaked coconut

Preheat the oven to 350°F.

Prepare the cake: Cream the sugar and shortening. Add the eggs and mix well.

Sift the flour 3 times and place in bowl with the cocoa and salt. Starting and ending with the dry ingredients, alternately add the dry ingredients and the buttermilk to the egg mixture, combining after each addition. Add the vanilla and the food coloring.

Dissolve the baking soda into the vinegar. While still bubbling, add this to the batter.

Pour into two 9-inch, well-greased cake pans.

Bake 25 to 30 minutes. Test with a toothpick to see if it's done.

Prepare the icing: Pour the flour into a medium-sized pan, and gradually pour in the milk. Cook over low to medium heat stirring constantly, until thick. Remove from the burner and cover with wax paper.

In a bowl, cream the shortening with the sugar and vanilla. Whip in the milk-and-flour mixture.

When the cake is cool, ice the cake and cover with the coconut. (For those allergic to coconut or who simply don't like it, you can leave it off, but our family doesn't think it's the same without it.)

 ## KAREN STALEY'S
CHOCOLATE WAFFLE

1. Take a frozen Eggo waffle (any flavor). Put in the toaster until . . . not frozen.
2. Put the waffle on a plate (or a paper towel in a pinch, 'cause you're going to wolf it down in a matter of seconds anyhow, so why dirty a clean plate?)
3. Go to the freezer.
4. Take one big scoop of Ben & Jerry's chocolate ice cream, and put it on top of the waffle. (Any brand of will do, but Ben & Jerry's is the best and probably runs neck-and-neck with Godiva's new ice cream for the most calories.)
5. Sit down by the TV and watch your favorite show, or just stand over the sink and devour this haute cuisine.
6. Take a nap before your blood sugar drops.

BECKY HOBBS'S
BECKAROO BROWNIES

These are dark, rich, KILLER brownies. For serious chocoholics only!

6 squares unsweetened chocolate
1½ sticks butter or margarine
6 eggs
3 cups sugar
1½ cups flour

1 teaspoon salt
1 tablespoon vanilla
1 cup chopped pecans
Powdered sugar

Preheat the oven to 325°F. Line a jellyroll pan with foil or parchment, then spray lightly with cooking oil. In a saucepan or double boiler, melt the chocolate and butter together over low heat. Set aside. Beat the eggs and mix in the sugar, flour, salt, and vanilla. Stir in the chocolate mixture and the nuts. Pour into the pan. Bake for 25 minutes, just until the top is dry. Cover immediately with plastic wrap and put in the freezer. After frozen, uncover, and sprinkle the top with powdered sugar. Cut into squares, and then cut diagonally. These can be made several days in advance and kept in the freezer until ready to cut.

LES KERR'S GRANDMOTHER'S
CREOLE PECAN PRALINES

Pronunciation guide: For those of you not from the Gulf Coast or New Orleans, praline is pronounced "praw-leen," not "pray-leen."

3 cups brown sugar
¼ cup butter
2 tablespoons whipping cream

1½ cups pecan halves
Cinnamon to taste

In a medium saucepan, combine the sugar, butter, and cream. Cook to a soft boil. Remove from heat. Add the pecans and cinnamon and beat until almost cold. Drop by the tablespoonful on waxed paper and let set.

RECIPES AND TIPS FOR THE CULINARILY CHALLENGED

 ## MARC BEESON'S "RECIPE"

Take 1 empty room; add 2 songwriters, 2 guitars, 30 ounces leaded coffee, 4 ounces nondairy creamer, 2 dirty jokes, and 1 great idea; stir gently. Let sit at room temperature for 3 to 4 hours. This should yield at least one solid verse and chorus and several trips to the john.

 ## MARCUS HUMMON'S KITCHEN TIPS

Recipewise, I only know a few things, and I cling to them like a lifeline.

1. Always put a touch of vanilla in your pancake batter, and *always* use Bisquick.
2. Always put the refried beans on the side, not in the quesadilla.
3. Put a dab or splash of water in your eggs when you make omelets.
4. Bananas and tomatoes are perfect primate foods.
5. Brie and apples are perfect picnic foods.
6. Finally, always use a pat of butter and a can of milk, not water, in your tomato soup.

 ## MARK JORDAN'S KITCHEN TIP

Here's a great way for the chef to have a good laugh in the kitchen. To avoid your eyes tearing or burning when you cut an onion, put a spoon in your mouth, concave side down. Voila! No tears, and it also provides a source of endless mirth for any guests who might be hanging around. Bon appétit!

CHAPTER 11

CAN'T BE REALLY GONE

The Bluebird has made a lot of friends in the twenty years we've been in business. It's a sad and inevitable fact that you're bound to lose a few in that length of time. We've said good-bye to several songwriters, performers, employees, and Bluebird regulars. A Bluebird scrapbook would not be complete without remembering them.

———⟩◆⟨———

LENNY BREAU Darci Cotten, the wife of one of Nashville's best jazz guitarists, Richard Cotten, submitted this lovely tribute to Lenny Breau, the first friend we lost.

Nashville is used to seeing long lines outside the Bluebird Cafe, people waiting to hear the great music of the night. One special summer night, in July of 1982, was no exception. As a matter of fact, the house was packed to standing room only, including some of Nashville's best-known musicians. Word was out that world-famous Canadian guitarist Lenny Breau was playing. Onstage that night

Richard Cotten, owner of Nashville's Cotten Music, joins guitar master Lenny Breau on the Bluebird stage for a night of six-string wizardry.

with Lenny was his longtime friend Richard Cotten, one of Nashville's most respected jazz guitarists. The music that night was magic. There was a hush over the audience, and everyone stayed until the end. For those of us who were there, it was probably some of the best music we will ever hear.

In the early fall of 1984, once again the Bluebird opened its doors for Lenny. Amy hosted a very special evening for him. Long after the music started, people stood in line waiting to get in. It seemed all of Nashville's musicians turned out, and a good number of them took the stage. This time, however, it was a memorial tribute to Lenny, to help pay his funeral expenses. Great musicians played, and we laughed and cried and remembered Lenny. He died on August 19, 1984. The police called it homicide.

My husband, Richard, died in July 1995 from leukemia. Perhaps Lenny and Richard share a different stage now. Those of us who heard them play their music were indeed fortunate.

DARCI COTTEN
September 4, 2000

———◆———

B. W. STEVENSON is best remembered for his big hit "My Maria" in 1973. He also penned the Three Dog Night single "Shambala." He passed away in April 1988. A few weeks after his death a tribute concert was held at the Bluebird with Townes Van Zandt, Mark Germino, Rodney Crowell, and Guy Clark among the performers.

—⇒◆⇐—

CHRIS AUSTIN was a member of Reba McEntire's band. A respected songwriter and multiinstrumentalist, Austin was on a plane that crashed in March 1991, claiming his life along with six other members of Reba's band and her road manager.

—⇒◆⇐—

RALPH VITELLO came to Nashville from Youngstown, Ohio, and found one of his first gigs on the road with Stella Parton. He was also a member of Jay Patten's combo, the very first band to play the Bluebird Cafe. A heart attack silenced this piano man in June of 1992.

—⇒◆⇐—

STORM SOMMER worked for us as a barback while attending college. We remember him as upbeat and free-spirited. A fall while hiking ended his life in 1991. He was only twenty-one.

—⇒◆⇐—

DAVE ALLEN was a big, jovial man with an infectious laugh. He wrote the number-one bluegrass hit "Blue Train" and also had a hit with the Forrester Sisters' single "I Got a Date." Cancer claimed his life in September 1992.

—⇒◆⇐—

ERNEST CHAPMAN was married to Beth Nielsen Chapman. He was diagnosed with a rare form of cancer in the early nineties and succumbed to the disease in August 1994. Beth's album *Sand and Water* is a moving tribute to their relationship and her own grieving process. Elton John adopted the title track as his live tribute to Princess Diana.

━━◈◆◈━━

TED HAWKINS was a busker on the streets of Venice Beach, California, before being discovered by Geffen Records. His first major-label album, *The Next Hundred Years*, was a soulful masterpiece. A stroke claimed his life on New Year's Day 1995.

━━◈◆◈━━

MAMA PRICE: Known around Nashville and the Bluebird Cafe as "the best friend a songwriter could have," Mama Price was one of a kind. Her real name was Marilyn Price, but to the countless songwriters she championed, she became "Mama." Her archive of pictures taken at the Bluebird is almost as extensive as our own. Her love for  music and the songwriter was boundless. She passed away on July 15, 1994. A memorial service was held at the Bluebird shortly thereafter.

━━◈◆◈━━

PEBBLE DANIEL was with us from day one. Her husky, blues-soaked voice was a highlight of every anniversary bash and Christmas show right up until her death on December 4, 1995. She was an original member of Jimmy Buffett's Coral Reeferettes and also performed with artists such as Crystal Gayle, Eddie Rabbitt, Tammy Wynette, and Delbert McClinton. She released albums on RCA and Elektra Records. She also contributed the song "Love Won't Come" to Tracy

Nelson's album *I Feel So Good*. Amy has described her as being "feminine, earthy, and tough—a real soul singer." Indeed, that was Pebble.

———◆———

WALTER HYATT was as loved and respected as he was talented. That's saying a lot. In Austin, Texas, he formed the now legendary Uncle Walt's Band with David ("Thinking Problem") Ball and Champ Hood. Hyatt moved to Nashville in 1987 and continued to perform and write. One of his biggest fans was Lyle Lovett, who used to open for Uncle Walt's when he was an up-and-coming songwriter in Texas. Lovett returned the favor, taking Walt and his new band out on the road as *his* opening act. He also produced Hyatt's album *King Tears*. Walter was one of the 109 people who lost their lives when ValuJet 592 went down in the Florida Everglades in May 1996.

———◆———

COLLEEN PETERSON enjoyed a long and varied career. She was a member of the Canadian vocal group Quartette and also recorded several albums as a solo artist. She won two Juno Awards (Canada's Grammy) and toured with artists like Gordon Lightfoot, Bruce Cockburn, Tom Waits, and Ry Cooder. She also appeared on Charlie Daniels *Volunteer Jam* recordings. We lost Colleen to cancer in October 1996.

———◆———

TOWNES VAN ZANDT A legend in his own time. Steve Earle has often been quoted as saying something like, "Townes Van Zandt is the best damn songwriter in the world, and I'll stand on Bob Dylan's coffee table with my boots on and say that." We're not going to argue. His best-known songs are "Pancho and Lefty," "If I Needed You," and "To Live Is to Fly." His songs were covered by Emmylou Harris, Merle Haggard, Willie Nelson, and the Cowboy Junkies, among others. Most of his own recordings were made for smaller independent labels. That changed after his death, when Arista Austin released *A Far Cry from Dead*. The title might seem a little ironic, but it actually makes perfect sense. Though a heart attack took his life on New Year's Day 1997, his music and his spirit are still very much alive.

DALE FRANKLIN was the transportation-and-lodging director at the original Woodstock in 1969. She brought that experience with her to Nashville in 1977, then branched out in the eighties, founding the Nashville Music Association, which would later become the Nashville Entertainment Association. In 1989 she cofounded Leadership Music and was the organization's first executive director. Her energy, insight, and passion have brought countless professionals together and shown them how to work with new ideas, clearer visions, and deeper commitment. She died of cancer in December 1994.

ROY HUSKEY, JR., carried on in the tradition of his father, Roy Huskey, Sr., and became one of Nashville's most respected acoustic-bass players. He played on numerous albums and was a member of several well-known bands, including Emmylou Harris's Nash Ramblers. He was voted Bass Player of the Year by the Bluegrass Musicians Union in 1990, '91, '92, and '93. He was just forty years old when lung cancer took his life on September 6, 1997.

JOE COMPITO A wonderful bass player and luthier, Joe Compito was never seen without a smile on his face. He made two basses for Victor Wooten of Bela Fleck and the Flecktones. As a player, he was best known as a member of Don Williams's band as well as Wild About Harry. A brain aneurysm felled him in January 1999.

DARRELL GARDNER was an unmistakable presence at so many of the Bluebirds' shows. His boisterous personality and booming laugh lit up the room as soon as he snuck through the back door to down a few Stoli's and confer with Mark Germino. A car wreck took him from us in July 1999.

FRAN MONTGOMERY Mother of singer-songwriter Nancy Montgomery and a Bluebird regular, Fran Montgomery was a fan of so many Bluebird artists. Her smiling face was a welcome sight to Bluebird performers as well as staff. We lost her in the summer of 1999.

⋙◆⋘

MARCIA WOOD was an in-demand session vocalist who also toured with artists such as Leon Russell. After retiring from the road she went to work for the Tennessee Film Commission. Her daughter, Heather Routh, works with us every year during our series of benefits for Alive Hospice. Marcia was also a regular performer at our anniversary and Christmas shows. We lost her to cancer in January 1999.

⋙◆⋘

DANNY MAYO Danny was the writer or cowriter of some of the most loved songs in country music. They include "Jesus and Mama," "Keeper of the Stars," and "If I Didn't Have You." His daughter, Aimee, is also a hit songwriter. Danny passed away on October 2, 1999.

⋙◆⋘

JIM VARNEY was best known as Ernest T. Worrell, star of *Ernest Goes to Camp* and a host of other Ernest movies as well as many Purity Dairy commercials. But he was also a songwriter, stand-up comic, and a serious actor who longed to break out of the country-bumpkin typecast that his alter ego had him locked in. That wish was almost fulfilled. Shortly before his death on February 10, 2000, he'd finished shooting *Daddy and Them* with Billy Bob Thornton and Laura Dern.

⋙◆⋘

LYNN SHULTS was, among other things, the man who saw Garth Brooks at the Bluebird and persuaded Capitol Records to give him a deal. His career began at Acuff-Rose Publishing in the sixties. In addition to working for several record labels, he also went on to cover the country-music industry for *Billboard Magazine*. He died in March 2000.

≋⟫◆⟪≋

JORDAN FIELD was only eighteen years old when a car wreck claimed her life. She had performed numerous times at the Bluebird, moving from the Sunday-night writers' showcases to longer sets during our early shows. Her younger sister was also seriously injured in the accident that took place in December 2000.

≋⟫◆⟪≋

JOHN JARRARD was an inspiration not just to songwriters but to everyone he came in contact with. His perseverance, good cheer, and optimistic outlook were tireless as he battled diabetes. Even as the disease claimed his eyesight and his legs, John continued to write chart-topping hits and light up every room he entered. "Money in the Bank," "Blue Clear Sky," "Sure Can Smell the Rain,"  and "Is That a Tear?" are just a few of the hits written by Jarrard. We lost John in January 2001.

≋⟫◆⟪≋

We support Alive Hospice. Over the years this wonderful organization has helped many people associated with the Bluebird deal with losing a loved one, and was indispensable when our waitress Liz Veitch was helping her brother, Billy, cope with the final stages of cancer.

OTHER CLUBS TO KNOW AND LOVE

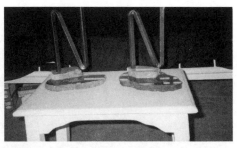

These funny-looking trophies are Nammies, given out at the Nashville Music Awards. The Bluebird was named Outstanding Music Club in 1995 and 1999.

We like to think we're the best listening room in the world (and we are), but we're certainly not the only one that caters to the songwriter. All over the country there are clubs that give folk, acoustic, and country songwriters a place to nurture their skills. Bluebird regulars have appeared at many of the following rooms.

⤜ THE BOTTOM LINE
New York, New York
The Bottom Line is our sister club in the Big Apple. Amy and Bottom Line owner Allan Pepper are in constant communication about shows and various talents. It's a great room for songwriters and original music. Definitely a must when visiting New York City.

⤜ CANAL STREET TAVERN
Dayton, Ohio
Many of the folk acts who tour the country make a stop at the Canal Street Tavern, either coming to or going from a Bluebird gig. We've taken the Women in the Round to this music room and recommend the venue all the time to other traveling troubadours.

⇛ CLUB PASSIM
Cambridge, Massachusetts

Passim is a Boston institution. For over thirty years it's been THE place for up-and-coming performers in that city's ever-fertile folk scene. Bob and Rae Ann Donlin helped so many artists make the leap from local hero to nationally known talent. The room is now booked by Tim Mason, who also handles the Old Vienna Koffee Haus in Westboro, Massachusetts.

⇛ THE ARK
Ann Arbor, Michigan

This Ann Arbor mainstay seats over four hundred people since moving to its new location in the heart of the business district. It's a non-profit organization and has featured all the biggest names in folk, rock, country, and blues.

⇛ THE TROUBADOUR
Hollywood, California

When the Grammys left New York City and went back to L.A., Amy didn't miss a beat, putting together another great night of nominees and thrilling the audience at this popular writers' hang in the City of Angels.

⇛ FREIGHT AND SALVAGE COFFEE HOUSE
Berkeley, California

This room has been around for over thirty years. It truly is a coffee-house—there's no alcohol and no smoking. (How folk can you get?) Located just outside San Francisco, the Freight and Salvage seats about two hundred.

⇛ BE HERE NOW
Asheville, North Carolina

There's a great folk and new-acoustic scene around the Asheville area. This is another great room we recommend to artists on tour. The Grey Eagle in nearby Black Mountain is also a fine venue.

⇝ OLD TOWNE SCHOOL OF FOLK MUSIC
Chicago, Illinois

One of our first "Bluebird Takes Flight" events happened here. Schuyler, Knobloch, and Schlitz took the In the Round experience to this venerable Chicago landmark.

⇝ EDDIE'S ATTIC
Decatur, Georgia

Just outside Atlanta in the lovely suburb of Decatur is one of our favorite writers'/acoustic-music rooms. Proprietor Eddie Owen is a true friend of the songwriter. He's nurtured many of our favorite talents, including Shawn Mullins, the Indigo Girls, Don Conoscenti, and Pierce Pettis.

⇝ POOR DAVID'S PUB
Dallas, Texas

There are many, many rooms to list in the great state of Texas, especially in Austin, Dallas, and Houston. Poor David's is one of our favorites. The Dixie Chicks first tested their musical wings in this popular Dallas venue.

⇝ THE SWALLOW IN THE HOLLOW
Atlanta, Georgia

The Swallow in the Hollow began when Bill Greenwood and Paul Doster spproached Amy about bringing some of the Bluebird's finest writers to their barbeque establishment just north of Atlanta. Always happy to share the wealth of talent in Nashville, Amy began sending our best and brightest in groups of threes to do shows on consecutive Friday and Saturday nights. It's been a complete success. This 175-seat club is almost always sold out.

FINAL THOUGHTS

This book was most definitely a collaborative effort. The initial idea came from Mark Benner. He began compiling stories and recipes as well as sending out letters to songwriters asking for their favorite Bluebird memories. Becky Hanover, one of our sound engineers and part-time office staff, stepped in and helped with the letter-writing campaign.

I came along after most of the letters had been collected and began editing them and placing them in appropriate chapters. We didn't really do too much editing; Amy wanted the voices of the various writers to come through.

Mark had already started going through the many photo albums we have in our archives. Amy and I began to choose the ones that best represented the stories. Virtually all the pictures were taken by Bluebird employees. And not a professional photographer in the bunch!

Along the way, Suzanne Spooner and Fran Overall, the Bluebird's office staff, were very helpful when we had to drag out a stack of photo albums or scrapbooks to look for a certain photo, calendar, or news clipping.

Freelance writer/publicist Mike Hyland also contributed valuable input throughout the process of putting this book together.

Without a doubt, there is another book that could be written with the stories we didn't receive and the few we left out to protect the innocent. Or guilty, as the case may be. This is the first edition. We hope you enjoy it, and we hope there'll be many more.

NEIL FAGAN
March 2001

So, for their stories, friendship, and support, we say thanks to the writers, performers, musicians, staff, and patrons who made this book possible. And for making the Bluebird Cafe the best listening room in the world.